FITTING IN &
STANDING OUT

A SMART WOMAN'S GUIDE
TO BUSINESS SUCCESS

Jill DeBok

Talonia
BOOKWORKS

FITTING IN & STANDING OUT

Copyright © 2016 by Talonia Bookworks, LLC
All rights reserved.
First Edition, 2016

Formatting by Rik – Wild Seas Formatting
(http://www.WildSeasFormatting.com)

ISBN 978-0-9971927-0-4

Talonia Bookworks, LLC
www.taloniabookworks.com

To all of the future female leaders just starting their careers in the business world - and the current female leaders still finding their way.

Table of Contents

INTRODUCTION - THE RELUCTANT TRAILBLAZER 1

ONE - IT'S A FACT, MEN AND WOMEN ARE DIFFERENT 9

TWO - I AM A FEMINIST, AND I BET YOU ARE TOO 13

THREE - THE NEED FOR SUCCESSFUL WOMEN IN BUSINESS 17

FOUR - WOMEN AS LEADERS 21

FIVE - SILENT MESSAGES 29

SIX - CONFIDENCE CRISIS 33

SEVEN - PERFECTIONISM IS A PROBLEM... 39

EIGHT - MEN ARE FROM MARS, WOMEN ARE FROM VENUS 43

NINE - GOSSIP GIRLS 47

TEN - MEETINGS 53

ELEVEN - SPORTS AND BUSINESS.. 57

TWELVE - FEMALES AS NEGOTIATORS 61

THIRTEEN - RESPECT AND INFLUENCE 65

FOURTEEN - AN UGLY BABY... 71

FIFTEEN - MANAGE UP AND DOWN 73

SIXTEEN - SEVEN SECONDS 77

SEVENTEEN - MISS MANNERS 81

EIGHTEEN - LOVE YOUR CLOSET 85

NINETEEN - YOUR PROFESSIONAL IMAGE 93

TWENTY - THICK SKIN 97

TWENTY-ONE - THERE'S NO CRYING IN BUSINESS 101

TWENTY-TWO - MANAGING EMOTIONS 105

TWENTY-THREE - BEING A "WOMAN" 111

TWENTY-FOUR - THE WIVES... 113

Twenty-five - Finding Support 115
Twenty-six - Make Life Easier 121
Twenty-seven - Two Drink Max! 131
Twenty-eight - Avoiding Sexual Advances.. 135
Twenty-nine - Discrimination And Sexual Harassment 139
Thrity - Safe Travels 145
Conclusion - A Bright Future For The Next Generation 149
Special Thanks 153
Bibliography 155

** This graphic indicates that gender differences are discussed in the next paragraph **

INTRODUCTION

The Reluctant Trailblazer

Today, I am a Fortune 50 executive and a single mom. I consider both to be great accomplishments.

Like you, my career began shortly after finishing college. With an undergraduate degree in Psychology, I had prepared for a career in social services. I quickly learned that my industry of choice would not pay my bills or offer job security, and so I changed plans and looked for a "real job" with a company that could employ me through my retirement.

My corporate career began in the early 1990s working for a large consumer packaged goods company (CPG). I was quickly recognized as an "up and comer" (up and coming executive) or a "hi-po" (a high potential candidate), and my career has moved at a very fast pace ever since. I stayed at that company for three years then left to pursue a graduate degree. Before completing that program I accepted a job offer from a competing CPG company, and I still work for this company today. (Since then, I completed my MBA.) Over my 20 plus year career path, I have held

14 positions with progressively increasing responsibilities in multiple areas including a call center, street level selling, distribution operations, high level strategic selling, marketing, general management and several leadership roles. Due to mergers and acquisitions, I have technically worked for four different CPG companies. And, thanks to the diverse companies that sell our products as part of their business model, I have worked with many industries: grocery, convenience and gas, major league sports, movie theaters, schools, vending companies, healthcare, and hospitality among them. While I earned a master's degree in Business Administration degree, many of the lessons I have learned in business were from "the school of hard knocks." My career has been a continuous learning path as I constantly prepare for the next role (or the role after that). It has been fast and fun and challenging every step of the way!

My industry involves manufacturing and shipping as well as selling and is physically demanding, thus very male-dominated. When my career began in the early 90s, women were not particularly visible in this business world. Women worked for the companies but in "female-friendly" support roles such as secretaries or receptionists; women were rarely in leadership roles or high-impact roles. I had very few women to look to for guidance. Forced to find my own path, I made plenty of mistakes. But, I didn't waste them. My mistakes were great learning experiences and often pole vaulted me into a new way of thinking which would help me, or create a "rule" for me to follow that would prevent a future problem.

Fitting In and Standing Out is a collection of those workplace experiences and my advice for you – business woman to business woman. It discusses important topics that help us understand why women often struggle in male-dominated business environments and how to successfully compete against male peers. More importantly, it offers advice on how women can work within the male culture without abandoning female strengths such as collaboration, communication and empathy. Awareness of the differences between men and women in the workplace - and yes, as we shall see there are some which could be barriers - is an important first step. The better equipped young women are to recognize the potential barriers, the more able they will be to remove them.

My psychology degree has benefitted my business career. My ability to observe and understand behaviors and social groups has been a great foundation for success. Sociology taught me that social groups are everywhere, a basic part of life, and that includes the business world. Our actions, thoughts, and beliefs are often guided by society or the groups that we associate with. So as my career began, being accepted by my new work group was important. Sharing a sense of unity and common identity with my co-workers wasn't about conforming to be like a man; it wasn't about gender. I just wanted to be a part of the team, to be successful and prove that I was capable and committed, not because I was a woman just because I was an employee. I had to stand out within the organization in order to get promoted. As it turns out being a woman, among other things, helped me stand out. My career success developed from both my ability to fit in and my ability to stand out. The goal of writing this book is to help you do the same. Being a part of the male/business culture and standing out in a positive way ensures that the people who are making decisions about your future will consider you to be a part of the team *and* a future leader.

I would be remiss not to mention that some feminists disagree with my approach. Because men continue to dominate business leadership roles, some believe that men continue to favor and promote those who are similar to them (other men) and that this reinforces the stereotypes and inequality. Some believe that men should change to accommodate women instead of women adapting to men. I agree with the theory. I just don't think it's realistic. It isn't fair that women bear the burden of adapting, but we will get further faster if we do.

I realize now that by learning how to fit in and stand out, I was a trailblazer - although I was a reluctant trailblazer. My formal education provided a great foundation, but my skills which allowed me to successfully work with men while being a female were self-taught. I never planned to pave the way for other women, and it never occurred to me that young women would follow my footsteps wanting to know how I succeeded. But today, I recognize the importance of my path and I want to help young women. My hope is that tomorrow's female leaders can learn from my stories, avoid my mistakes, and benefit from the advice I offer. I want to make the business world easier for them because I was there and because I shared my stories.

In today's world, women are better represented than ever before. It is so exciting and encouraging to witness the changes. Young woman today are more likely than men to complete college and attend graduate school. Young women today have a wide range of careers available to them, and today's corporations are working hard to develop their talented, young female employees to prepare them for future roles as leaders within their organizations. Many companies offer special female programs that focus on inclusion, career development, formal presentation skills, networking, developing a personal trademark, and other valuable training, but I would argue that these lessons are valuable for *all* young professionals. There is a need to address some very real topics that prevent women from furthering their careers. As women, let's talk about these issues rather than shy away from them. Let's ignore political correctness and support each other. Let's look at the gender stereotypes, recognize the truth to them and consider ways to work around them. Let's take advantage of our strengths in the workplace and advocate for ourselves and each other.

Women are fairly well represented at lower levels of business, but as the corporate ladder rises, women become less so. As recently as 2012, 90% of CEOs were male. Clearly there is more work to be done, and in my view we are avoiding some tough topics. Corporate training programs are not telling women how to mitigate the common female challenges such as lack of confidence, the drive for perfectionism, an unwillingness to delegate and how our biology drives our emotional expression – all of which comes down to this: *how* to successfully work alongside men. When young women in my organization ask me for advice, they ask about very real challenges, and many of these challenges are specific to women. How women handle these situations determines how the men they work with regard them, how much respect and influence the women will have from the men within the organization, and whether or not male superiors will support the women for advancement.

This book shares tactics that young women can use to be a part of the male-dominated business world and stand out in it. While the feminist movement has accomplished many things, women still struggle in the business world. Women have special issues to deal with that men simply do not. Young women need to develop unique skills to successfully work alongside men which will insure their careers have a chance to progress to all levels of the business world.

Here's to STRONG WOMEN. May we Know Them. May we Be Them. May we Raise Them.

~ Author Unknown

You have to learn the rules of the game. And then you have to play better than anyone else.

~ Albert Einstein

I don't mind living in a man's world as long as I can be a woman in it.

~ Marilyn Monroe

ONE

It's A Fact, Men And Women Are Different

The Declaration of Independence says, "All Men are created equal," and the Fourteenth Amendment of the United States Constitution guarantees "equal protection of the laws." Equal and equality mean that people have the same value, not that people are the same.

We like to think that gender stereotypes are invalid, simplistic descriptions, but the reality is that most people do share the characteristics of their gender stereotypes. We know that men and women are different. Differences between the sexes have been consistently found across cultures, life spans and species. Ignoring these differences and their impact on business relationships will not make it easier for women to gain better positions in the business world. Ignoring the fact that the business world (like society) views these gender stereotypes *unequally* is the heart of the issue for women in business. The business world is a patriarchal society where men still dominate and masculine traits are considered more highly valued; therefore male characteristics are more highly rewarded with promotions and financial compensation.

Biological and cultural forces impact how a person's gender develops. Both are powerful influences. Some feminists believe that gender is completely socially created, but many scientists disagree. While male and female genetics are 99% the same, the one percent of differences are significant and wide-ranging: structural, chemical, genetic, hormonal and functional brain differences.

Hormonal influences are a significant difference between men and women. Hormones determine what the brain is interested in doing, and males secrete higher levels of testosterone while females produce more estrogen and progesterone. Testosterone has been linked to risk-taking, assertiveness, masculinity and feeling powerful, all of which are rewarded in business. The female's primary hormone, estrogen, is known to fluctuate with her monthly cycle leading to the stereotype that women are moody and emotional, which is "not good" for business. Women also produce 52% less serotonin, the hormone that controls anxiety, than men and have a larger cingulate gyrus which is a small area of the brain that some refer to as the "worrywart center". Estrogen also encourages bonding and connection and supports the areas of the brain that involve social skills and observations, which are good for business. There is no question that the male and female hormones impact the gender stereotypes.

Beyond hormones there are some other biological differences between the sexes –

specifically the way the brain operates. Intellectual ability does not differ between the sexes, but brain imaging technology shows that men and women use different parts of the brain to process the same information, and males and females maintain their unique brain characteristics throughout life. Male brains are about ten percent larger than female brains (brain size does not correlate to intelligence), but men lose brain tissue three times faster than women as they age. MRI images also show that men and women differ in how the brain is used. The brain is divided into two hemispheres. The left side controls the right side of the body and is responsible for language. The right side of the brain controls the left side of the body and handles emotions. Generally speaking, men use one side of their brain, usually the left, while women use both sides. There are also two types of brain matter, gray and white. Men have more gray matter, which is used for isolated problems, and women have more white matter, which is used to integrate information. Female brains are more active with 30% more neurons firing at any given time than men. All of these differences between male and female brains lead to female strengths: looking at the "big picture," multitasking, communication, empathy and social thinking, intuition, collaboration, self-control, memory and emotional expression. The differences in brain activity also explain why men outperform women on spatial skills, learning and performing single tasks, math skills, pain tolerance, risk taking and coordination. Girls are wired with girl brains, and boys are wired with boy brains. The question scientists still debate is whether the sex differences in the brain are present at birth or if they develop with socialization (nature versus nurture).

Many of the gender stereotypes are supported by science. Male and female behaviors and personalities can at least be partly explained by the variations of hormones and the utilization of the human brain between the sexes. Men and women *are* different. These differences don't have to divide us, but we should talk about them and what they mean for women in business.

TWO

I Am A Feminist, And I Bet You Are Too

Feminism is another topic that can be divisive in the business world but doesn't have to be. When I think of a feminist, I think of an abrasive, angry woman. Abrasive and angry women are not successful in business. I am a feminist though, and everyone I know is a feminist. A feminist is a person who supports the belief that men and women should have political, economic and social equality. It is about empowering and celebrating women, but modern extremists on both sides of the political movement have given feminism a bad reputation.

Examples of feminist resistance against patriarchal oppression are evident at least as far back as ancient Greece. Plato's *The Republic* even states that women should work alongside men, receive equal education and share equally in all aspects of the state, but it was the suffrage movement, advocating women's right to vote, in the nineteenth century that is widely recognized as initiating the first wave of feminism. The second wave of feminism began with the publication of *The Feminine Mystique* by Betty Frieden in 1963. It was the voice of educated, white women, bored and isolated in suburbia, and subordinating their own needs to those of their husbands and children. The voice became a rally cry. New found attention to cultural and sexual inequalities lead to many positive changes addressing domestic violence, rape, family law, and the access to education for women. A new recognition of sex discrimination began, and many national women's organizations began to form, such as the National Organization for Women, simultaneously with the civil rights and anti-Vietnam War movements. The third wave of feminism is the contemporary division of feminism into three diverse categories. One category is gender-reform feminism which emphasizes the similarities between men and women with the goal of women having the same opportunities as men. Another category is gender-resistance feminism which argues that women should break away from male dominance and form separate women-only organizations and communities. The third category is gender-rebellion feminism which focuses on the interrelationships among inequalities of gender, race, social class and sexual orientation as one piece of a complex system of social stratification. Each of these three groups of feminism has sub-groups resulting in many diverse, and disagreeing groups. Today's feminism is a fractured political environment which has deteriorated support of the movement particularly among a younger generation of women who came of age later, indifferent to or ignorant about the workplace issues their mothers and grandmothers battled. In today's world, the word "feminist" has a very negative connotation, but I do believe in political, economic, and social equality for women, therefore I am a feminist, and I bet you are too.

I call feminism to your attention because I'm sure you are apprehensive about using the term. As a collective group, today's women can rebrand feminism. We are not oppressed. We are not subordinate. Feminism earned us the right to vote, equity in education, and continues to give us equal opportunities. As you approach the business world, know that you are a feminist, and assume the leaders you work with are too. They will support your professional development equally with your male peers.

THREE

The Need For Successful Women In Business

When I think of diversity and inclusion in business, I often think of a marketing class I took during graduate school. The topic was marketing blunders. Intentional or not, the professor made a compelling argument for the need for diversity while he gave examples of tragic advertising mistakes companies made out of ignorance. Companies failed to communicate their message and in many cases were outright offensive because they lacked cross cultural understanding. One classic example involved the Ford Motor Company. They had a model called the Pinto which had poor sales when it was introduced in Brazil. It was later discovered by the company that the word "pinto" was a Portuguese slang term for "tiny male genitals." Diversity within their organization would have mitigated Ford's embarrassment. This example and many others illustrated that companies need broad cultural understanding.

For our purposes, the business world needs to include the diversity women represent for many reasons.

Businesses perform better when they include women. Women are terrific communicators, typically better than men with both written and spoken words. Clear communication is critical to drive revenue, control costs, manage talented employees, and build strong customer relationships. Networking is another natural strength for women and increasingly important in business today with expanding global networks. The diverse viewpoints women offer in business become important when decisions are being made and innovative solutions are needed. Building relationships is another skill that is instinctively easier for women and very important in retaining talented employees and when collaborating with customers. The talent pool doubles when females are included and increased competition will continue to require new thoughts in business. Women also tend to be better multitaskers than men, advantaged at juggling many tasks in rapid succession which is helpful in fast-changing, competitive business environments. Women have valuable and natural strengths which are beneficial in business.

Furthermore, research shows that companies with women in leadership roles prove to be successful. A 2014 study revealed that companies with 1000 employees or more and a female leader generated 18% more revenue than businesses lead by men. Another study comparing Fortune 500 tech companies found that businesses with three or more female senior leaders had a greater return on investments then male-led companies. Gallup found that companies with more diversity had 22% lower turnover and an easier time recruiting other diverse candidates. Businesses which include women in key roles are better equipped to meet the needs of the consumer market. Women impact 85% of purchasing decisions, roughly equaling $4.3 trillion dollars of U.S. consumer spending, making American women the largest single economic force in the world.

With all of these facts about the benefits companies receive when there is a female-inclusive environment, it is difficult to understand why women still struggle to be equally represented and equally rewarded in business. A 2015 survey found that gaps between men and women in business are still very real. Today, women make $.77 cents for every dollar a man makes. Men tend to have more responsibility with budgets two times larger than women's and men benefit from three times the administrative support. But the young women entering the business world today are changing those numbers. Millennial females, with higher education than their millennial male peers, earn $.93 for every dollar a millennial male makes. Inclusion of females in business is progressing, even if the change is slow.

FOUR

Women As Leaders

When my career began, few women were in leadership roles, but that is changing too. Effective businesses today are lead with collaboration and cooperation which is great for women because that is the natural way we lead. Authoritative, command and control cultures are becoming a thing of the past. Today's leaders are competent, qualified visionaries who also empower their people and look for consensus. The corporate world is ready for women to lead.

First, let's consider the differences between management and leadership. Today's companies are actively looking for leaders, but the truth is that a good company needs a balance of both. You will likely have to be a successful manager before you have the opportunity to be a formal leader. Managers and leaders are complimentary systems. Management is about practices, policies and procedures, and leadership is about creating culture and coping with change (change in technology, competition, government regulations, strategy, etc.). Leaders come in all shapes, sizes and temperaments, but effective leaders have two things in common -- results and ethics. Leadership is a fascinating topic with literally thousands of books discussing how to identify and develop the requisite skillset. Leadership is the process of inspiring, influencing and guiding others to a common goal with the use of authority and social skills.

In *Breaking Through "BITCH" – How Women Can Shatter Stereotypes and Lead Fearlessly* Dr. Carol Vallone Mitchell discusses the challenges females face with leadership and how leadership is different for men and women. With her "Women's Leadership Blueprint" Dr. Mitchell outlines nine key competencies that successful *female* leaders embody:

- **Achievement drive**: the inner drive to achieve more than what is expected
- **Conceptual thinking**: the ability to see relationships and connections that help others understand parallels
- **Confidence**: a strong belief in personal ability coupled with sharing authority and power
- **Cultural and political savvy**: an understanding of cultural and group dynamics and adapting to work effectively within the system
- **Inspiring commitment**: the ability to create a sense of belonging and loyalty within the group

- **Persuasion**: the ability to connect core values in order to influence others
- **Self-development savvy**: taking responsibility for getting appropriate developmental experiences, exposure and career growth
- **Strategic control**: maintaining control of initiatives while being collaborative and delegating and empowering others
- **Tempering assertiveness**: creating a sense of relatability and approachability while being assertive by using humor, empathy and common ground

Dr. Mitchell's comments on the differences in successful leadership between men and women resonate with me. Recently, I participated in a training class which required me to take a personality test, the Myers-Briggs Type Indicator (MBTI). The MBTI looks at the way people use their perception and judgment, based on eight personality preferences people use at different times, and then our class looked at how those individual preferences apply to organizations, to our organization specifically. I found out that I am an extrovert who is energized by the outer world, rather than an introvert who prefers an inner world. I organize information and make decisions based on feelings and values, rather than logic. My perceptions are based on intuition, rather than using my five senses, and my lifestyle is organized and planned, rather than spontaneous. I was pleased with this analysis and agreed with the interpretation of myself. But, I was surprised to find that none of my peers shared these same preferences, however, I was also the only female in the panel. The biggest difference was that only one of my colleagues and I make decisions based on feelings and social values. The rest of the group organized information and made decisions in more logical and objective ways. Our class facilitator explained that 60% of the people tested who have this preference for feelings and social values are females while only 40% are males. Most men, and most business leaders, make decisions based on logic and objective truth.

This difference in decision making between the sexes explains why my male counterparts do not see the world the same way I do, and they do not think about the same things as they make decisions which was very interesting to me. As I thought about the findings I realized how important it is for me, a female leader, thinking about the health of our organization, to express my opinions when I disagree with our decisions. Most of our decision-makers are using logic to make decisions, but making decisions based on feelings and values is especially important around initiatives that directly impact employees. As a female leader, I know that I think about decisions differently, and I need to share my thoughts and opinions with the other leaders instead of letting a lack of confidence make me think I am wrong because I disagree. I have a responsibility to the organization to ensure we are thinking about our decisions from all angles to make the best decisions we can. This is the exact reason so many organizations today are striving for diversity. Organizations need diverse thoughts to make the best decisions.

My personality results, which indicate I prefer feelings and social values over logic, coincide with the fact that female leaders seek employee buy-in. We excel at creating consensus, getting everyone on the same page, as well as working to achieve mutual goals. We have an inherent ability to listen, a concern for relationships, and teamwork and a more natural ability to compromise for the good of the whole. We excel at making employees feel recognized and rewarded. These are the traits corporations are looking for with their future leaders, and they are the same strengths Dr. Mitchell points out in her book.

Women have some challenges with leadership also; delegating and giving feedback, for instance, which are also critical in the business world, go against our female nature.

Women have a natural tendency toward perfectionism and empathy which can make it difficult for us to delegate. Sometimes we think we can do it better ourselves or that it's just easier to do it ourselves rather than coaching someone else on how we want it done. And, women are good at understanding and feeling what others are experiencing. This can make it harder for us to add to someone's workload if we think they already have too much going on. Women should think about this differently. Showing people you trust them is a great compliment and stretching their boundaries helps them grow. Not to mention, there will be times when you need help and support from others to manage the workload. Delegating also means you can genuinely include others in your success which women like to do, so the challenge for women is to reframe how we think about assigning work to others. When to delegate is an important consideration. Here are some key questions to ask yourself:

- Is there someone else who has the knowledge and expertise to do it? Or, is it critical that you do it yourself?
- Does the task provide a learning opportunity for someone else?
- Do you have enough time to delegate the task effectively?
- How problematic would failure or missing the deadline be?

If you decide to assign tasks to others, keep these tips in mind:

- Be clear about the expected timeline and outcome.
- Be transparent about constraints. Discuss who has the authority, responsibility and accountability.
- If needed, allow other tasks to be reassigned to help the person you are delegating to.
- Assign tasks to a person close to the work at hand.
- Provide support when needed, including your

availability for ongoing communication.
- Focus on results rather than detailing how the work should be done.

While delegating can be difficult for women, so can giving negative feedback, especially in a very competitive work environment. In business, feedback is essential to success. People need feedback in order to improve. Women are naturally good at giving positive feedback but feedback on areas for *improvement* can be difficult for us. We worry about the reaction from the employee and how to correctly frame the conversation for corrective action. Think about these tips when giving feedback for improvement:

- Give specific examples of what needs to be improved.
- Discuss the issue(s) needing work in a timely manner, before poor habits are formed. Not addressing an issue makes it look like it is accepted.
- Women tend to soften feedback sessions with compliments. Be careful with positive comments during a conversation about improvements that need to be made. This can be confusing and deter from the corrective action you are seeking.

There is still an underlying bias against females as leaders in the business world. Traits that come naturally to men such as assertiveness and confidence are the qualities people still attribute to leadership.

The traits more natural to women such as empathy, kindness and emotional expressiveness result in women being poorly represented in corporate leadership roles, but the tide is changing as women are now known to be better leaders overall. It is important for females today to understand the differences between male and female leadership and what we have to offer an organization: competence as well as nurturing qualities. Many people believe that women are better leaders because of our natural communication skills and our preference for teamwork. Our time to be more equally represented in leadership roles is coming.

FIVE

Silent Messages

Our personal belief systems influence our thinking on how women fit into the business world. So what influences a woman's personal belief system that drives her to want success? Have you thought about what has influenced you to become the woman you are? Do you dream about the woman you want to be? Have you thought about your courage and personal power and where it comes from? Many young women ask where I found the strength to have the career I've had. The question surprised me the first time it was asked. After reflection, I realize that I was fortunate to have several strong female role models while growing up. Watching them, I received their silent messages about what it was like to be a woman.

My mom was single in the 1970s, raising three kids largely on her own. She worked very hard to provide for us, as a grocery store cashier and as a clerk at an insurance office. She did whatever she could to keep us going. She believed owning a house and having a home for my brothers and me was one of the most important things she could provide as a mother. She reached out to a realtor who told her she would need to put 50% cash down and show 6 months savings because banks wouldn't give mortgage loans to single women back then. I witnessed her work ethic, and I experienced her struggle when she could not provide the material items for us that we wanted. But my mom scrimped and saved, and in 1977 she did purchase a home for us. Later, she became a real estate agent, determined to help other women like her. My mom taught me the connection between hard-work and personal rewards.

Maureen, my future step-mother, had a "man's" job at the phone company. She was a pole climber. In the 1970s all phone lines were above ground, so people who worked for the phone company would climb poles to hook and unhook (literally) phone lines when anyone needed to start and end phone service. It was a tough and tiring job, going up and down poles all day and an outdoor job, no matter what kind of weather. I thought Maureen was cool! She was pretty, smart and easy to talk to. She shared her work stories with me too, which was interesting because other adults did not talk to me about work. And, she talked to me about the men she worked with because they stressed her out *every single day*. They would not be her friend, simply because she was a woman. It hurt her feelings and made her angry at the same time. She talked to me a lot about being a woman in a man's world. She loved her work, and she was good at it; and she liked being outdoors and physically active. She talked to me about her strategy to handle the men which was simply to blend in and not call attention to herself. She believed that she should look as masculine as possible so she wore little to no make-up and kept her hair short. That was how she avoided verbal abuse from them, and when the men were hateful, she ignored them and did the job she was paid to do.

Another strong female in my family was Aunt Stacia. She influenced me more than I understood as a child. She was my grandpa's sister and rumors circulated the family that she and her husband had been bootleggers during Prohibition, running moonshine back-and-forth between Chicago and St. Louis. I was enchanted! By the time I came along, Aunt Stacia was old and frail. She taught me that women could have great, unknown strengths.

Then there was Grandma Ruth. She is the nicest woman in the world. She was a single, career-woman in the late 1940s before the church introduced her to my grandpa and the married when she was 35 years old. To this day, I am compelled by her years in business and amazed at how courageous she was to live so differently than the other women of her era. Grandma Ruth taught me that strength and independence can be beautiful and kind.

So as I grew up, the women around me were strong. Women did what they had to do to take care of themselves and their families. Women operated within the world of men by playing by the rules and fitting in. Women had strength, beauty and kindness. That is what I was taught, and that is what I expected of myself. What are the silent messages guiding your belief system around being a woman? And how does that influence your ambition? What messages will you send to your family?

SIX

Confidence Crisis

This is tough to admit, but I lack confidence. As I said, my career has moved quickly. You would think that would make me self-assured, but it has been the opposite. Confidence comes from experience and knowledge and allows you to act and speak without self-doubt. As I moved from position to position, never doing any one job for more than two years, I never had the luxury of being confident. I was ALWAYS learning. I never felt like an expert. Even today, as I transition to the role of the veteran, I am always learning and stepping outside of my comfort zone. My role continues to change as I continue to cover larger territories, learn about different customers and new marketplaces. Confidence can be hard to achieve when you are constantly learning new things. But, confidence in yourself, confidence in others and confidence in your organization are three critical requirements for a successful career.

Recently, I attended a developmental meeting for female future leaders at our company. In the course of our discussions a resounding theme that came from the meeting participants was a need to develop self-confidence. Time and again the subject came up – how to gain it and why it impacted almost every aspect of our work. Even though I felt I secretly lacked confidence too, this bothered me. These women were invited to this meeting because they are our future leaders, the future leaders of a Fortune 50 company. They are smart, talented, driven women - how could so many of them lack self-assurance?

So, I began doing some research, because I wanted to understand why so many high-achieving women, including myself, lack confidence and what we could do about it. It turns out that lack of self-assurance among females is widely recognized. Women blame themselves when things go wrong and don't take credit when things go right. Evidence shows that women are less self-assured than men. And studies show that *success correlates with confidence as much as it does with competence,* not a good correlation for women as future leaders. The research also tells us that compared to men, women think they will score poorer on testing, generally underestimate their abilities and do not consider themselves promotable while men *overestimate* their abilities and performance.

Confidence is visible. Body language communicates self-assurance or a lack of it. People instinctively read non-verbal cues to judge if a person is confident, capable and ready to work. Building self-confidence will help you be successful and help you prepare for your future. The "talent" that companies are searching for is really a combination of competence and self-assurance. Speaking clearly, answering questions assuredly and admitting when you do not know an answer is viewed as confidence and demonstrating these skills will make it easier for you to influence others and appear more competent. Others will have a difficult time believing in you if you fumble, cannot find your words or act nervous.

Confidence requires a growth mindset. New skills can be learned which lead you to do new things and built self-assurance. There are skills women can learn to help master self-confidence which will improve the perception of competence. Here are some tips to develop your self-confidence:

- **Self-awareness**: think about all of your accomplishments and strengths and write them down so you can refer to them when you need a confidence boost.

- **Set achievable goals**: set targets for yourself that utilize your strengths and measure yourself against them. Identify the small, achievable steps you can make and acknowledge your progress as you build real confidence.

- **Positive thinking**: think positive thoughts and do not give in to negative self-talk. In fact, talk back to the negative thoughts in your head and tell them why they are wrong.

- **Take action**: nothing builds confidence faster than doing things and learning from the experience *even if you fail*. If you grow and improve, you will gain confidence.

- **Be prepared**: preparation brings me

confidence more than anything else. The more anxious I am about a meeting or presentation, the more planning time I allow.

- **Dress for success**: when you look better, you feel better. Plan your wardrobe to project the right image. (This is discussed in more detail in Chapter 18.)
- **Body language**: instantly demonstrate that you are self-assured by presenting yourself with your head held high, good posture, a relaxed demeanor, and very important, don't forget to make eye contact.
- **Be authentic**: do not try to play a role. Just be you.

Displaying confidence, and competence, does not mean you pretend to know everything. No one knows everything, and most people dislike others who act like they do. But, successful people surround themselves with other successful people, so make sure you align yourself with that group.

I was a sorority girl, and "rush week" – experiencing it from both sides – taught me some unlikely business lessons. In a perfect world all of the girls in the sorority could meet all of the girls rushing the house. But, there are too many girls rushing in a very short rush week for that to work, so we developed a system. We hid notecards and pens under sofa cushions, behind furniture, in books on shelves, anywhere we could quickly grab them. After we met a girl we would pull out our notecards and pens, make a few notes about our thoughts on the girl we had just met then hide the notecard and pen again quickly and wait to meet the next girl. Then at the end of the night we would review each girl as a group. The girls who met the potential pledges would refer to their notecards and report their impressions of each girl to the group. When it came time to vote on which girls would be invited to join the house, only girls who met the pledges would vote. The girls who had no information about the potential pledge would "trust the sisters," acknowledging that they didn't know enough about the girl to say if she should be invited into the sorority. In business today, I think of this often when I recognize that others are in a better position to make a decision because they know more about a topic or situation. I trust my colleagues when I am not the expert. Trusting those with the most knowledge to make the best decision empowers the organization, ensures good decision-making and fosters a healthy culture.

I have also expanded this thinking to "trust the system." A young female future leader in our organization recently asked me for career advice. She was offered a promotion that she did not feel she was ready for. I shared with her that I had often felt the same way. But, I always accepted the roles that were offered to me anyway because I had nothing to lose and much to learn. The worst thing that could happen was that I would lose my job, and I knew that I could always get another. Today as a leader, I know that organizations do not offer promotions to people who cannot handle the role. Sometimes the organization will take a chance on a person if the job is a stretch, but they do not intentionally set anyone up for failure. The leadership team always sees something in the candidate they believe will lead him/her to success or they do not offer the job. Most companies would turn to an external candidate or restructure the role if no internal candidates can handle the job. Today, I understand all of the work that good companies put into talent identification, developing future leaders and succession planning. My advice to the young woman was to trust the system and take advantage of the opportunity.

Confidence is dynamic. It comes and goes with different circumstances. It is related to self-esteem, optimism, self-compassion and self-efficacy, all of which are important for a healthy personal and professional life. Confidence may continue to be a work in progress, but confidence in yourself, in others and in your organization are three critical requirements for both fitting in and standing out in your organization.

SEVEN

Perfectionism Is A Problem

Voltaire is credited with saying, "Don't let the perfect be the enemy of the good." Women are more likely to be perfectionists than men because it is tied to a lack of confidence. Perfectionism comes from being overly critical, either of oneself or of others. A lack of confidence leads perfectionists to constantly make unfavorable comparisons of themselves and/or the team and to set unrealistically high expectations. At its best perfectionism will help you achieve your goals, but at its worst will drive you to become a harsh critic with unattainable goals and lead to depression, low self-esteem and poor work relationships.

When I think of a perfectionist, I think of Natalie Portman in the movie *Black Swan*. Her character was an obsessed and dedicated ballerina, trying to meet the demands of her mother, herself and her director. In the short term, perfectionism worked for her, but in the long term it destroyed her.

Dancers are known to be perfectionists in their craft, but in business perfectionism can diminish a person's performance. The need to be perfect actually makes people less productive because time gets wasted on minute details, and tasks are made to be more difficult than they really are. Perfectionists often only see the details and miss the big picture. If the perfectionist is a manager, people will recognize him/her as a "micro-manager" instead of as a leader, which creates demoralizing and poor working relationships. Employees will see the leader as unrealistic, rigid and inflexible.

Female perfectionists have additional challenges. According to research, we are less likely to advocate for ourselves when seeking a promotion or a raise unless we are 100% sure we meet all of the qualifications for it while men advocate for themselves when they are only 50% sure. As female perfectionists, we doubt our opinions, over-think and over-analyze. We are harder on ourselves than circumstances warrant.

Are you a perfectionist? Here are some questions to ask yourself:

- Are you detail oriented and highly critical of mistakes?
- Do you aim to be the best at everything, even when it's something you are not interested in?
- Do you make deep personal sacrifices (sleep, meals, family time) to complete tasks flawlessly?
- Are you absolute (black and white, no grey area) in the way you see your work?

- Are you too harsh a critic of yourself, fretting over even small mistakes?
- Do you mull over outcomes that did not turn out the way you planned?
- Do you fear failure and become defensive with constructive criticism?

Overcoming perfectionism does not mean giving up on your goals, it means giving up an unhealthy obsession and not getting hung up on things that are out of your control. If you think you need help, use the following strategies:

- Assess your tasks and decide which ones really make a difference in the bigger picture. Only those that have wide impact deserve the extra time and energy your perfectionism longs to give.
- Delegate work to capable employees and coworkers and let them do it, no one likes to be micro-managed and it does not help people grow.
- Accept mistakes from yourself and your team, learn from them and move on. Stop obsessing over what could have been different and stop assigning blame. Focus on what can be done now.
- Stop getting lost in the details and keep your eye on the bigger picture.

- Celebrate victories and progress. Reward yourself and your team when the job is well-done and give credit when deserved.

Setting high standards and putting your best foot forward are commendable, but perfection is not attainable and really has no value. As an employee, being a perfectionist will actually make you less effective. As a leader, perfectionism will backfire when your employees feel undervalued and untrusted, plus it's exhausting and you will wear yourself out. Do not let perfectionism be your enemy of good.

EIGHT

Men Are From Mars, Women Are From Venus

John Gray, Ph. D wrote his classic *Men are from Mars, Women are from Venus* in 1992. This enormously popular book discussed the vastly different communication styles between men and women. Written to help couples with their personal relationships, these differences also carry into the professional world. Men take charge with their communication while women encourage collaboration. Men listen with minimal eye contact and offer little verbal feedback which women interpret as not listening because women use eye contact and visual responses as a way to show they are listening. Men will often continue to talk when someone tries to interrupt, talking right over that person and not letting them speak, while a woman will be polite and defer to the other person. (I do not stop and let people interrupt me anymore. It is a power play, and I find it rude, but it is how the game is played, so I play it.) Men are also more comfortable standing side-by-side while women are more comfortable face-to-face, so men sometimes interpret face-to-face conversations as confrontational. When a man nods, it means he agrees, but when a woman nods it means she is listening. Basic communication techniques vary markedly between the sexes.

Men and women also have different strengths and weaknesses in their communication styles. Men tend to be direct with their interactions and their use of body language. Women are good at picking up non-verbal cues, listening and displaying empathy. Men struggle sometimes because they are too blunt, insensitive or too confident. Women's modes of communication can be overly emotional, meander and lack authoritativeness. The differences are important to recognize so that you interpret situations correctly.

You may need to develop skills to communicate more effectively *with* men. You can do this by focusing on several things:

- Learn how to banter, without flirting. These friendly insults are actually considered compliments by men which can help you bond with them.
- Participate in sports conversations (sports and business are discussed more in chapter 11).
- Monitor your body language and use your physical presence to establish your position.
- Speak concisely; avoid rambling and fillers like "um" and "like."
- Think about your comments and questions

before you engage in a conversation or enter a meeting.

- Ask questions to make sure you understand the other person's point of view.
- Repeat what the other person said to clarify your understanding.
- If someone confronts you or insults you, agree with them in some way. Validating the perspective, expertise or feelings will soften their position and bring them to your side. You can say, "I agree that this is a problem, this is how I'm thinking about it." Or "Yes, that was a difficult decision. Let me give you the background."

Communication is one of the biggest differences between men and women. It impacts how we interact at the office, how we build interpersonal relationships and how well we fit in with the company culture. By being alert to the differences and monitoring how your communication style is working for you, you can make some adjustments and turn communication into a real strength.

NINE

Gossip Girls

We know that communication styles are different between the sexes, and it is widely believed that women have better language skills. Right or wrong, women also have a reputation for sometimes using those language skills to gossip. It comes from our need to be a part of our community and to protect it. Men rarely gossip about their concerns. I did not understand this difference when my career started.

A year after I graduated from college, I found my first "real" job. It was an entry-level position with a Fortune 500 company, and I was very excited. I felt honored to be selected because I knew there many other talented young graduates who would love to have the opportunity I had been given. My mom helped me buy new, professional clothes. I got a haircut and bought fresh make-up. I was ready for my future to begin!

So, on the very first day I was surprised to hear my boss, Jennifer, say, "Just do your job and keep out of the gossip, and you'll have a great career here."

What? Of course, I would stay out of the gossip. I didn't even know anybody who worked there. And, the secret to success had to be more about working hard and working smart, didn't it? Why hadn't she talked about results? And teamwork? And a positive attitude? I was not impressed with this new Fortune 500 boss of mine...she had pretty low expectations, I thought.

Today, I will tell you that Jennifer's instruction to me that day was one of the best pieces of advice I have received over my long career. I now understand the wisdom she spoke. It is amazing how many people actually don't *just do the job and stay out of the gossip*. Some people are lazy, some procrastinate, some have difficulty working with others and being on a team; others are unable to focus on the task at hand. But it's also amazing to me how much time people spend gossiping in their offices or in the hallways, rather than getting their work done.

Gossip includes talk about the company or other individuals. Company talk about potential layoffs, mergers, promotions and the company's economic health can hurt morale and reduce productivity. Gossip about other people can make it an unpleasant and insecure work environment. Gossip reduces productivity simply because of the time it consumes. A 2002 survey estimated employees spend 65 hours a year gossiping at work.

As it turns out, there have been a lot of studies about women and gossip. Women gossip for several reasons and it actually has some benefits:

- Gossiping helps us process, dissect and understand the experiences we have.
- It is a way of fitting in and connecting with a co-worker because it shows that you trust the person you are confiding in.
- Many believe that gossiping reduces stress because hearing about another person's problems can make people feel better about their own challenges.
- Gossiping helps women validate feelings and gain perspective.

Feeding gossip and workplace drama is always a poor career choice, and it's why some men think they can't work with women. It's important, however, to recognize the informal structure of an organization. Companies invest considerable resources on their formal structures (as laid out on organizational charts) but it is often the informal networks that are the heart of a company. Informal networks are the relationships that employees form across functions, divisions and local teams. They are a naturally forming social network that connects employees. The same relationships that can get you into trouble with gossip can also provide you with valuable insights and important allies.

"Cliques" have a bad reputation, but people naturally fall into groups. So, it makes sense that it happens in the workplace just like it happened in high school. People naturally bond with others viewed as similar to themselves. In the workplace you can benefit from being in the clique as long as you do not alienate others who are not. And, you want to make sure you are joining the right clique, the one with leaders and future-leaders. Informal networks are a great source of information, again, as long as you are tied to the right clique. And, they are a great source of quick feedback. These networks can also help you ask questions and gain insights across functions. When people feel personally connected to you, they will be more collaborative with you.

The watch-out of informal networks is that they can also lead to gossip, inner-personal conflicts and poor use of time. Here are some tips on how to stay out of the gossip.

- Stay busy so you are unavailable to the gossipers.
- Don't listen or participate. Politely excuse yourself from the conversation.
- When someone else is being negative, turn the conversation by saying something positive.
- Keep your private life to yourself.

As it turned out, I did follow Jenifer's advice, just do my job, and stay out of the gossip, and it has been a great path to success. Being a part of the team is important, and it makes work more pleasurable. You need alliances, to connect with others and to be a part of the network where information is shared and opinions are formed. Informal networks are the pulse of the organization, just avoid the gossip.

TEN

Meetings

Mondays are brutal. My first meeting is at 8:00 a.m. and I typically have five additional internal meetings on any given Monday. We review the prior week's performance and the new week's priorities with various teams across our organization. At each meeting I have numerous files and spreadsheets to refer to in order to accurately speak about the current business trends and our go-forward strategies. Being organized is critical, having the data, knowing where the data is, and being able to quickly find the information demonstrates solid business acumen.

On Sunday evening I review the final numbers from the previous week's performance, compare it to our prior year's results as well as to the forecast we had committed to. I gather my thoughts for the upcoming week's priorities and plan my topics of discussion on each of the Monday calls. On Monday morning, I arrive at the office 30 - 45 minutes before the first meeting to finish my preparation. When I go into my first meeting, I sit in my regular seat. In the past, I had my files organized in clearly labeled file folders which were neatly stacked so I could quickly grab whichever resource I needed.

I changed this practice a few years ago after reading an on-line article. The author claimed that a woman's use of space at the conference table speaks to her confidence and her sense of entitlement to be there. Thinking about my stacked files at my first meeting every Monday morning, and comparing that to the man I always sat next to whom always used lots of space, the author's comments resonated with me.

As women, we tend to be naturally polite and considerate of other people. This carries over into the business world, but politeness and consideration are not necessarily viewed as strengths in business. Politeness and consideration can earn you friends, but it can also override our ability to assert authority and power in the business world. Politeness and consideration of others can lead us to be small and meek in our space too. Women should spread out and take the room at the table needed for files and resources. Business meetings are important and, like her male colleagues, a woman has to speak correctly and confidently at the meeting. So today, if you sit in on one of our Monday morning meetings, you will see me with my laptop open, my iPad open and my hard copies of files spread out around me, easily accessible. They are no longer stacked up in a tight, compact pile waiting for me to sort through them.

In fact, physical presence is widely recognized as a key difference between men and women in the business world. Men tend to be taller and larger than women and we generally equate mass with power, so men gain an instant sense of presence that women do not have. You can compensate by standing tall with good posture, broadening the stance, putting your hands on your hips while standing, and putting your hands on the desk while sitting, to take up more physical space. Also, remember that women are perceived as less professional when we twirl our hair, play with jewelry, cross and uncross our legs, and so on. Be mindful of your physical stature and body language.

Men also have deeper vocal tones than women. According to research, men use only three tones. Women use five vocal tones, and our voices rise under pressure, making us sound more emotional. If you and I were in a meeting together or on a conference call, you might notice that I control the pitch of my voice because a lower voice commands more respect. And, female voices do not carry as far as male voices. Be sure to speak loud enough for the farthest person away to hear you.

You will also notice that I am very punctual, but this was not always the case. I learned this from my teenage daughter. The dance school she attends insists that "On time is late -- to be punctual is to be 15 minutes early." If dance class starts at 4:00 p.m. then she is expected to be there at 3:45 p.m. so that she can put on her dance shoes, stretch and be ready to begin at the start time. I started applying this lesson to business, and I was amazed at how much easier my days would go. By getting to a meeting BEFORE it starts instead of when it starts, I can network and gather my thoughts before the meeting begins. An unexpected benefit is that I love the social time punctuality offers. When meeting a customer for lunch or a drink, I used to arrive at the meeting time. Now, I arrive 15 minutes early, use the restroom, get the table and review my presentation. The same is true for conference calls. Now, I always dial into a conference call two minutes before the start time. This allows me to be on for the roll call and not miss anything. Sometimes the conversations before the meeting are just as valuable as the conversations that take place during it. I have also learned to use the restroom before any conference call or meeting. Stepping out is always rude, and if you are uncomfortable, you will be distracted from the business at hand.

Meetings are a critical part of business. The men and women you work with will think more highly of you if you use the space you need, use a strong voice, are ready to begin at start time and do not need to step out of a meeting. Being prepared for the meeting and being a part of the conversations is critical to fitting into the organization.

ELEVEN

Sports And Business

It is impossible to talk about the differences between men and women in the business world without talking about sports. As I was growing up in the 1970s competitive sports were barely available for me to play. Girls could enjoy cheerleading or square-dancing – seriously! In 1972 Congress passed Title IX which opened the doors of education and athletics to women, but that law was not enforced until 1980 with the formation of the Office of Civil Rights. Many argue that Title IX still needs attention and revisions today as women continue to face obstacles in higher education, athletics and employment.

Today in the United States, men play sports three times more often than women. Advocacy groups believe gender has no bearing on sports interest, but studies report otherwise. The American Time Use Survey found that 51% of all exercise is performed by women but only 24% of that involves participatory sports. Another study observed public parks in 4 states and found that 37% of the exercise participants were women but only

12% of the team-sport participants were women. And a third study of intramural sports at colleges and universities found that only 26% of the registrants were women. So, even with the efforts of Title IX, women engage more in exercise than sports and more men participate in sports than women.

These imbalances carry over into the business world. My company works hard to be an inclusive organization, still every meeting and every conference call begins with banter about the latest televised sporting event. Like many other women of my generation, I am not interested in sports. I usually do not know what they are talking about so I politely listen and wait for the conversation to be over.

These sports conversations are a constant reminder to me that men and women bond differently. Men bond with banter, silence and an activity:

- **Banter**: banter is a friendly use of humor as insults.
- **Silence**: men do not need to talk in order to bond. In fact, fishing, watching T.V. and doing other activities together without talking is a way they show support for each other.
- **Activity**: men get together around a purpose (help fix a car, build shelves in the garage, golf, fish, etc.). Women can get together just to talk.

Businessmen, and business women, also bond on the golf course. Because of my career, I have learned to play golf. Golf is a great way to have a five hour business meeting with key customers, where you can get in valuable networking time, build relationships and share information while enjoying the outdoors on a nice day. If you are not a great golfer, I encourage you to play anyway. Most golf outings are charity golf tournaments, "scrambles" where each team uses the best ball played throughout the course. This way of playing is preferable to me because I am not that good at golf. Keeping that in mind, I have several strict golf rules:

- **Look like a golfer**: most of the networking during a golf tournament takes place before and after the actual golf game itself. You will likely only golf with three other attendees, as a foursome, so as long as you look like you know what you're doing everyone else around you will assume you are at least okay at the game.
- **Avoid playing on teams with serious golfers who want to win the tournament**: my skill level does not support a serious game, so I always try to be on a "fun" team. My goal is simply to play well enough so I do not embarrass myself and enjoy the time the event provides for networking, building relationships and sharing information. In fact, most golfers fit into this category, so do not be overly worried about how well you play. Just try to be on a team that does not care.
- **Only discuss business that your customer (or employee or boss) wants to discuss**: never use

this time together as an opportunity to "drill" people with questions or "sell" something. The golfers will not want to play with you again, and you will lose valuable opportunities in the future for developing your business/career.

Golf outings are great opportunities to demonstrate that you are smart, competent and capable. Even if you do not play golf at all, you should still go to the tournament. You could volunteer to help which would certainly be appreciated, or you could just go to the event to network at the start or end of the event and offer a polite excuse to explain that you are not playing.

I do not begrudge the fact that sports are intertwined with business culture. I have done what I can to adapt. My lack of sports knowledge may have excluded me from certain conversations, but it has not hurt my career. I hope the benefits of Title IX will help the business women of the future participate more in these casual discussions and sporting events.

TWELVE

Females As Negotiators

Negotiation is a fact of life. We negotiate every day, whether it's personal or professional. In fact, most decisions are made through negotiation. You might be relieved to learn that there is absolutely no evidence that shows men negotiate business deals better than women. In fact, evidence shows that women *out-negotiate* men in most scenarios, yet females are often criticized for not negotiating for themselves.

The cost of *not negotiating* can be high in any deal, but not negotiating for your career and compensation package can literally cost you years of additional work. A lot has been written about the discrepancies in compensation between the sexes. Much evidence supports these concerns, and women are often blamed for not negotiating for themselves. In fact, many studies show that fewer women attempt to negotiate a job offer than men. And, people who negotiate their salaries get an average of seven percent more than people who do not. Moreover, that seven percent compounds year after year; its absence can add years to your work life before you can afford to retire.

Women are accused of not negotiating for many reasons. Perhaps we have lower expectations or worry that our (male) boss will penalize us and think we are greedy. Maybe we want to avoid creating conflict. Maybe we don't think we deserve higher compensation. Whatever the reason, our caretaking, communal nature makes negotiating for better compensation uncomfortable for us. We have no problem negotiating for our business or our family, but we resist negotiating for ourselves. Like any other negotiation, preparation is the key. Here are some thoughts to make you feel more comfortable:

- Use your network to research what others in your role are receiving for compensation. I would avoid these conversations within your peer group at your company, but counterparts at other companies would be a good reference. If you can't get the information through your network, consider speaking to a head hunter (recruiter) to see what you would be worth in the marketplace. Some people recommend you do this every few years as matter of practice.

- Think about financial considerations beyond base salary: healthcare, bonus, car policy, etc. and don't forget about tax implications.

- Negotiating with your boss includes more than financial compensation. Your career can also benefit from higher status, increased visibility and additional resources.

- Negotiating a larger salary will likely be easier during a transition to a new role or after you have received some business accolades, as opposed to a regular annual review. Assess the situation to determine if your timing is right.
- A soft approach will probably feel more natural. Think about framing your request around how you can help the organization and even your boss directly with additional support.

We negotiate in all areas of our life, and there is no reason to lack confidence in this area. Negotiate for yourself!

THIRTEEN

Respect And Influence

My first role in management was early in my career. I was a 23 year old distribution supervisor, responsible for managing merchandisers (general laborers) and union truck drivers. Many of the drivers had been with the company 25 years or more. They had been driving a truck longer than I had been alive, and now I was their boss. To say I had a challenge ahead of me was an understatement.

My first test came fast. I had only been in the role a week when I received a panic call from a sales manager who needed a merchandiser (laborer) to immediately go to a small grocery store nearby. The driver had delivered product which now needed to be added to the grocery shelves and displays. According to the union policy, I was instructed to offer a task which offered overtime pay to the drivers available in order of seniority. But, when I got the call, there was only one driver available which meant he would have to go. Little did I know, Daryl was a very senior truck-driver. This meant he typically drove the truck to stores where our product was unloaded for him with fork lifts. He did not actually have to physically work the cases himself anymore. When I asked him to go merchandise the store, he said he did not want to go, that I should ask the next driver who came in. I explained that he had to go because someone had to go, and he was the only one available. He was done talking to me and left the room, obviously upset. I assumed he had left for the store, and I did not understand why he was so upset because the union policy was clear.

Worried about the exchange, I decided to discuss what had just happened with my boss, but my boss was not available. So I went to talk to his boss who I found standing in the hallway talking with Daryl. Daryl was complaining that I was making him go back out, then he turned to me, and we were physically standing toe-to-toe. Daryl was eight inches taller than me, broad shouldered, clearly angry and very frightening. He was intimidating with his stern face and death stare, but I stood my ground, making direct eye contact and waited for someone to speak. The executive spoke, and he said, "Daryl, you need to go to the store. You can file a grievance though," and Daryl went to the store. I was shaking on the inside but no one could see it. I was worried that Daryl would file a grievance because I honestly still did not understand why he was so upset. But I was also glad my boss' boss backed me up. Word traveled quickly throughout the organization. No one could believe I had made Daryl go merchandise a store. Daryl did file the grievance with the union, but he lost, and I finally figured out that I had insulted him by asking him to merchandise the store. He was "better" than that (more experienced, more senior). But, my encounter with Daryl was a great learning experience for me as a new manager. He eventually got over it, and I earned respect from the other drivers and supervisors for following and enforcing the rules. No one ever questioned me again when I asked them to do something, at least not in that role.

Your job title alone will not win you respect from your organization – you have to earn it. Here are six ways to earn respect:

- **Be authentic**: be yourself and people will find you trustworthy.
- **Be open-minded**: ask questions and listen to what people have to say.
- **Be discreet**: don't gossip, and keep the secrets others share with you. Be someone people can confide in.
- **Be consistent**: consistency translates as being fair to employees.
- **Be helpful**: contribute to the success of the company and help others achieve their goals.
- **Set boundaries**: set limits so you can honor your commitments.

For women working in a man's world, earning respect is very achievable. It really is as simple as being authentic, discreet, open-minded, consistent, helpful and following through with commitments, and that is true for all levels of an organization. And, it's important because after you earn respect, you can start influencing others. With respect, people listen when you speak and they take action when you request it. Your ability to influence others will make you stand out in your organization.

Influence is an essential component of leadership because it leads to business results. Leaders influence in multiple ways based on the task at hand and what they need to attain. Aristotle identified three tools for persuasion: logos, pathos and ethos.

- **Logos (logical)**: logical appeals are rational and intellectual arguments which gain alignment with ideas and goals because they simply make sense. They sound like, "Based on our financial analysis, this is our best course of action."

- **Pathos (emotional)**: emotional appeals promote a feeling of well-being or sense of belonging to gain support. Others agree because the requested action meets individual goals and values. An emotional appeal would be similar to, "This plan is a slam-dunk for our talented and competitive organization. If we can't get it done, no one can!"

- **Ethos (ethical)**: ethical appeals build a connection based on character and experience to gain support of a proposal. An ethical appeal might sound like, "I have worked with this customer for almost a decade, I am confident this is the right strategy."

When you are facing a situation where you know you need to influence others, plan ahead. Set your goals, think about the audience and determine your influence strategy. With practice and experience, your persuasion methods will become smooth, comfortable and natural.

Respect and influence are intertwined, but respect comes first. Respect is earned regardless if you are a woman or a man, and it is the first step of persuasion and influence. Whether or not your job title gives you authority, earned respect and the ability to influence others will give you power and help you stand out to the leaders of your company.

FOURTEEN

An Ugly Baby

At one point in my career, my company really struggled to operate. Because of a poor leader, we did not have the tools and resources we needed to do our jobs. Our employee turn-over was high. Our equipment was unreliable. We did nothing in the name of good customer service.

Coincidently, I had a customer, Rich, who was experiencing similar issues within his organization. He worked for a large national retailer as a District Manager and Buyer, responsible for about 30 stores in our area. One day, Rich and I were visiting stores together. The whole day was designed to help us both – to help me sell my products within his stores and for his stores to sell more products in general (including mine but not just mine). We both wanted to increase sales. It should have been simple, but it was a depressing day for both of us. I was embarrassed; we went to several stores where my company had not delivered items that were advertised in the stores' weekly circular. Rich was embarrassed, how could his stores not have my nationally recognized products, whether or not they were featured in the weekly ad?

At the end of the very long day, he looked me straight in the eye and said, "This might be an ugly baby, but it's our baby! We are going to take care of it and watch it grow!" And, we developed a plan – a plan that grew our business monumentally. I was even recognized nationally as "Vendor of the Year" all because I took care of my ugly baby, and I watched her grow.

This was my first lesson in "owning my business." Like it or not, good or bad, I was responsible for our business with that customer, and it was my job to fix it. I couldn't let it overwhelm me, I couldn't accept poor results, and I couldn't believe it was out of my control. I think about this often when I'm facing a challenging business situation. Rich taught me to see it, own it, solve it and change it. Our plan began with communication and the conscious choice to solve the problems. This ugly baby gave me a great opportunity to stand out in my organization. Taking responsibility for your business is critical to success.

FIFTEEN

Manage Up And Down

Clearly, an important key to success is to earn respect from across your organization. During your career it will be important to manage up and manage down, meaning work successfully with those lower than you in the organization as well as those higher than you in the organization. While managing up and managing down are both important, I know I am better at managing down which truly benefited me early in my career. Managing down simply involves being a team player, clearly communicating the priorities, being fair, listening, asking for input, and being available to the employees. These are all natural skills for most women. Managing down empowers and strengthens the team below you. My ability to manage down allowed me to work closely with the lower levels of the organization which gave me valuable insights to make good decisions. Our leadership teams saw this and identified me as a future leader.

Managing up has been a weakness for me just as it is for many women. I am not comfortable promoting myself, but managing up is important. It strengthens relationships with those above you and turns recognition into promotions. You can manage up without being boastful. Managing up includes juggling priorities correctly, producing results, understanding what your boss needs and wants from you, being proactive and keeping your boss informed on your work's successes and challenges. Here are some additional considerations to help you stand out with the leaders in your organization:

- **Toot your own horn in a way you are comfortable**: results may not matter if you don't communicate them.

- **Be visible**: put yourself in position to interact with the leaders of your company and get to know them. If you can't do this naturally at the office, make sure you participate in company events as well as community events and special projects your leaders are involved with.

- **No surprises**: become an expert over your business. Your leaders expect you to know what is happening. You should be the one to communicate bad news as well as good news regarding your area of responsibility. This is especially helpful when you can do it *before* a problem arises. Managing the expectations of your leadership team is a critical communication skill.

- **Don't "wing it"**: there is no greater or more permanent loss of credibility with upper management than by making up answers. It is okay to say "I don't know… let me get back to you," but it is not okay to give them the wrong information.

- **Forgive yourself when you make mistakes**: when discussing a financial mistake I made a few years ago, my boss said to me, "When you're constantly driving 100 miles per hour, eventually you are going to veer off the road." When this happens to you (and it will), accept responsibility, get over it and move on (but don't repeat the mistake).

- **Provide information, not reports**: demonstrate that you understand the information by providing summaries of reports along with the reports. Don't make people guess what you are trying to tell them by providing a bunch of data without an explanation. It's okay if they have a different interpretation, just share yours.

The highest end of managing up is having contact with senior leaders, especially if you work for a large Fortune 50 company like I do. Think of it as a job interview because it is, you just don't know what the job is or when it will be available. I didn't understand what this was about early in my career, so I want to explain it to you and spare you the angst I experienced. First, if anyone allows you to have exposure to a senior leader, it means you have been identified as a future leader and your bosses are confident you will not embarrass them in front of their superiors. This is a huge compliment, but also a huge responsibility. You probably won't have much presenting to do at your initial interactions but you should be prepared to answer some very general questions about your business. The senior leader will want to get to know you a little personally and professionally. You are there for a reason and you will not be ignored – which is what I thought my first time. I thought I could just be a fly on the wall and learn from being in the presence of the senior leaders, but I was wrong. Your single goal is to come across as competent, confident and someone the senior leader could see being a part of the leadership team in the future. The senior leaders simply want to confirm that you know your business, you are competent and you present yourself well. Be ready and you will be fine, they want to like you, they expect to like you, just don't mess it up!

Managing up and managing down are both important for your career development. At the end of the day, it's about being respectful and approachable to everyone. Believe it or not, that will make you stand out amongst your peers.

SIXTEEN

Seven Seconds

I'm sure that you know that you only have seven seconds to make a strong first impression, and you probably know that your smile, eye contact, body language and professional manners are critical tools. Woman to woman, I would like you to also think about a few other details.

A firm handshake with good eye contact communicates self-confidence. Right or wrong, women are perceived to have a weak handshake which signals insecurity. Make sure your handshakes are firm and appropriate. Here are some tips:

- If it's an introduction, wait to shake hands after you exchange names (so you can focus on the name and remember it).

- If you already know the person, usually the higher ranking person extends the hand first, but if you are not that person and the higher ranking does not extend a hand, then you can

extend your hand first.
- Always stand up for a handshake.
- Smile to communicate you are approachable and confident.
- Practice with friends and family to make sure your handshake is firm (not too weak, not too strong).
- If appropriate, add warmth or a more personal touch by putting your left hand on top of the other persons hand and gently shake.

Believe it or not, sometimes a hug is more appropriate in business than a handshake. I have customers who I have known over 20 years. If I offered my hand to them, they would be offended, too cold and impersonal. When I am with them, I offer a hug (if they do not). An appropriate business hug with a man is a half hug (only one arm extends around to the man's back). But, when hugging another woman, a two arm hug is appropriate. For a first introduction in business, I would stick with the handshake, but after that you will have to decide if a warm hand shake or hug is more appropriate in your business environment.

I also encourage you to think about your purse and workbag and the impression they give others. Businessmen seem to fixate on shoes as a status symbol, but for women purses and bags are a quick measure of social standing. As a female professional, your accessories make a powerful statement about who you are, and your purse and workbag are usually visible when you walk into a room. Make sure they reflect the quality and personality you want to project. Your purse and workbag should be clean, in good condition, the right size, so you have the items you need without the bag over-flowing, and proportional to your body. The quality of the accessories you carry should be sturdy rather than flimsy. That is, it should hold its shape. The straps should be long enough to easily hang on your shoulder but short enough that they do not drag against the ground if you carry the bag with one hand. And, color is also important. Your purse and work bag should be neutral or coordinate with your outfit and/or overcoat.

As women we also have to think about our nails. I was offended the first time I heard this. I thought it was very sexist, but now I agree. Dressing for success includes your total look and the details matter. Manicures and pedicures with open-toed shoes give the impression that you are pulled together, "finished," and well-organized. I stick with clear polish, nudes or light colors. Bright colors can be harsh and distracting and they can more quickly identify that my manicure is overdue. I also think embellishments such as jewels and special designs look less professional, but those decisions should be guided by what is appropriate for your role/industry. The point is to have a well-groomed appearance which includes your nails.

First impressions will be important throughout your career. Long after your job interview you will continue to meet new customers and colleagues. As a female keep your handshake, purse and workbag and nails in mind as you are projecting your image. The first impression you leave is a mini-presentation of you are as a person and the company you represent.

SEVENTEEN

Miss Manners

My boss, Keith, sends me a hand written note at the end of each year to thank me for solid results (or a solid effort if our year did not end as planned). I have a customer, Bill, who *always* sends a thank you note after my company entertains him at a sporting event or concert. The hand written notes from these two men (and the consistency of them) makes them stand out to me as kind, appreciative and courteous. Good manners simply show respect for others, and in today's rushed and stressed out business world, good manners will make you stand out amongst your peers. Even in our looser, less formal business environment, poor manners remain unacceptable. Business manners include many things. Remembering people's names (and details about their family), a handshake greeting, punctuality, putting away your hand-held devices so your attention is clearly focused on the person or people you are with and an efficient use of other people's time will all make you stand out as a professional person increasing your business success.

- **Remember names and family details**: mention the person's name 2 - 3 times during a conversation. It will help you remember their name and build rapport. Use "Mr." or "Mrs." until the other person tells you not to. This gesture will communicate respect. Also, when introducing people to each other, use the higher ranking person's name first.

- **Be presen**t: texting, answering calls, checking your email communicates that something else is more important than the person you are with. Multitasking is rude.

- **Respond quickly**: phone calls and emails should be answered on the same business day if received before four o'clock in the afternoon.

- **Do not abuse "open door" policies**: while many companies foster open communication with leadership teams, this is not an invitation to interrupt a meeting or distract someone working on a project. Even with "open door" policies, it's polite to schedule time for a meeting.

- **Be respectful of people's time**: time is valuable and no one has enough of it. Be organized and thoughtful when you are seeking their guidance or assistance, and always say, "thank you for your time."

Manners are a sign of professionalism, and having them will increase your success in the business world. Business manners include all of the common courtesies you learned as a child: please, thank you, excuse me, ma'am, sir, eye contact, a smile and table manners. Stand out amongst your peers by minding your manners.

EIGHTEEN

Love Your Closet

Early in my career, I saw our most senior female leader speak at an annual meeting. I was so impressed by her knowledge and presentation skills. She was brilliant, well-spoken and talented, but she also clearly appeared exhausted. Her hair needed a good cut and color; she needed some make-up to brighten and animate her face, and her wardrobe needed help too. In fact, her physical appearance actually made me question my career goals. Did I want to be that same haggard executive?

Fast forward a few years, I looked in the mirror and I realized that was just who I had become. My hair and skin looked bad and my wardrobe was frumpy.

Then, I read an interesting article in a woman's magazine which pointed out that movie stars look like movie stars because it is their job to look that way. Movie stars spend time, money and energy on taking care of their bodies, skin, hair and wardrobe. Even for movie stars, it takes work to look good. And that includes the rest of us. I realized I had not been investing my time, money or energy into my physical, and professional, appearance.

Shortly after I read that article and knew that I could be doing better, I attended a fundraiser where I purchased a mystery box. In my mystery box I received a gift certificate for a one hour consultation with a wardrobe stylist. Although I knew I needed help, I waited nine months before making the call.

Jennifer came to my house and we talked about my life -- how I wore clothes, what kind of clothes I wore and what events I needed clothes for. Then she looked at my closet...we spent an hour that day going through everything and getting rid of items that were too old for me, styles that were too young for me and anything that was worn out or looked cheap. More than half the clothes in my closet were put into bags to be donated or sold at a resale shop. Although Jennifer was kind and respectful, it was actually really funny. I could not defend, excuse or explain some of the clothes that were hanging in my closet, and I had very few accessories. By the time we finished that day, I recognized the value in the service and asked her to come back another time so that we could finish. Then, my teenage daughter "fashionista" helped me color-sort the clothes that remained.

I was starting to love my closet again, but now there were a lot of gaps in my wardrobe. So I met Jennifer at the mall. It was great; in less than 2 hours I had 10 new outfits with all the accessories. Jennifer knew the types of clothes I needed, the styles of clothes I liked and the sizes for what I needed. Before meeting me she had gone through the sale racks, the designer racks and the value racks to select dresses, slacks, tops and accessories that would work for me. At both the department store and the women's boutique we visited, she had filled a dressing room with racks of clothing, accessories and shoes laid out for me to try on. I have never shopped so productively! Jennifer was exactly what I needed, and I returned home with a new wardrobe that I immensely enjoy without a huge investment of time.

Jennifer taught me that every woman's wardrobe should really include three types of clothing: work, social, and household. Work clothes include business casual, business and formal. Social clothes include daytime and evening, and household clothes are more casual outfits that you wear at home or to run errands. And those outfits really do not intermingle, which mine used to do a lot! Here are the different types of business dress for Corporate America:

- **Casual Fridays**: jeans or knit pants can be worn. Always opt for a nice shoe such as loafers, ballet flats, or low wedges instead of a tennis shoe and wear a blouse instead of a t-shirt.

- **Business casual**: slacks or a knee length skirt and a blouse are appropriate for business casual settings; no jeans, no khakis and no golf shirts. In a more corporate setting add a sweater jacket or a business jacket. Do not wear a suit and jewelry should be light.

- **Business dress**: a suit is required for business dress. This may consist of a knee length skirt or slacks, but must always be worn with a long-sleeved jacket that matches and with minimal jewelry. Panty hose are no longer required for business dress. High heels, up to 3 inches, and open-toed shoes are acceptable. Invest in alterations if off the rack sizes do not fit your body nicely. Fit makes a huge difference no matter how expensive the garment.

- **Business formal**: conservative evening wear is acceptable. Think classic instead of sexy. Cocktail length is usually appropriate, and a basic black dress of good quality with sequined accessories is generally a safe option.

It is important to be thoughtful with your wardrobe and personal style in business. I am often amazed at how poorly some women dress at work, how many young women who do not know how to dress professionally. During the business day women should never wear embellished or beaded tops, shear tops which show undergarments, fishnet hose, tops that reveal cleavage or golf shirts (unless of course it is a golf outing). I have seen women wear what is essentially evening wear and club wear to the office. All of these wardrobe decisions absolutely lead to a lower level of respect from the organization.

Evaluate your business wardrobe for these basics, especially if you have a tight budget. Investing in the right pieces will stretch your wardrobe. You should have:

- Flattering pants, skirts, jackets and sweaters in

basic colors

- Quality, durable pieces you can wear often, including shoes and handbags
- Blouses, camisoles and layering pieces in neutrals
- Accessories and additional blouses and camisoles to add color and variety to your wardrobe

Here are three other quick ways to update your look without spending a fortune: invest in good alterations, a good haircut and new eyeglasses. If you are like me you may have a range of sizes in your closet (fat clothes, regular clothes, skinny clothes). Take some of your favorite pieces that currently fit poorly and have them altered so you can wear them. Your hairstyle is another easy update. A fresh cut in a current style and color will boost your ego and keep your look fresh. Invest in a great hair stylist and keep your hair appointments. In fact, never leave the salon without having made your next appointment. Eye glasses are another quick image-fix.

Accessories are really important. You need them to have a polished look, but wearing too many at once will distract from your professional image. Before I met Jennifer, I was lucky enough to be selected to attend a special training course. The class was about the "presence" of executive woman. We discussed how our physical appearance, presentation skills and communication style impacted the impression we left, which ultimately affected our careers. This is where I learned "the rule of thirteen" which simply says that a woman should not have more than 13 wardrobe items visible on her business appearance. So on a typical day, here are mine from top to bottom:

2 earrings

+ 1 necklace

+ 1 shirt

+ 1 sweater or jacket

+ 1 ring

+ 1 watch or bracelet

+ 1 belt

+ 1 pair of pants or a skirt

+ 1 purse

+ 1 work bag

+ 2 shoes

= 13 Visible Wardrobe Pieces

The point is to be feminine but not flashy in a way that your appearance detracts from your intelligence. Layering too much jewelry or over-accessorizing detracts from a professional appearance.

I love business dress for women today. It's okay to be feminine! When I started out, I was actually coached not to dress like a woman, to appear a bit masculine and to down-play my femininity. That was honestly good advice at the time, but I am glad things have changed. Today, women can wear open-toed shoes, pants, lace and pretty colors, but we must always remember to keep it professional, keep it conservative, and never wear evening clothes to the office. A women's wardrobe should never distract attention away from what she is saying.

So ladies, keep it tasteful and smart. If you find yourself in a fashion rut, you have to get out of it! Your appearance does impact your professional image and your credibility. If you find a great person like Jennifer to help you, so much the better. You deserve to look like the put-together professional you are, not exhausted and beat up by your job. Make sure your physical appearance, wardrobe and accessories project the image you want people to see. It matters!

NINETEEN

Your Professional Image

First impressions, manners and wardrobe all contribute to your professional image, but also much more. People are constantly observing your behavior and forming theories about your competence, character and commitment. All of these opinions translate to your professional image.

As a leader who participates in corporate succession planning, I can tell you one of the most common topics discussed is whether or not a solid performer has the presence of a leader, which translates to the potential to be a leader. It is not enough to be smart, experienced, results-oriented, collaborative and loyal to the company. You also must look like a leader and carry yourself like a leader in order to get promoted to be one. Someone with a good professional image (sometimes called "executive presence") projects self-confidence, takes control in uncomfortable situations, makes tough decisions, participates in tough conversations, demonstrates solid presentation and public speaking skills and has influence within a group.

Even if you do not dream of being an executive, your professional image impacts your future. To develop your leadership presence:

- **Look the part**: make sure your wardrobe, hair and overall look project the image of a leader in your company.
- **Communicate clearly and concisely**: effectively deliver information and engage others in conversation so you can listen and respond.
- **Be authentic**: be yourself and be approachable.
- **Develop formal presentation skills**: power point skills and conference room speaking will be important for an organization of any size.
- **Improve your public speaking skills**: speaking to a large audience of employees is inevitable for leaders of large organizations.
- **Keep your workspace clean**: whether you work from a cubicle, a car or an office, your workspace is a reflection of your ability to organize and manage your job.

Another consideration regarding your professional image is your personal brand. How do you want others to see you? How will you market yourself? Strong brands like Google and Mtn Dew have staying power and success in the market place. Many professional coaches advise professionals to think of themselves as a brand to be marketed within the workplace. What makes you stand out from others in the marketplace? How can you market those qualities? Many people develop an "elevator speech" to brand themselves and influence how other people see them. An elevator speech is a short statement about you and the value you bring to the company. You should take credit for your skills and accomplishments, align with company goals and sound conversational: with an easy tone, pitch, and volume. It should be comfortably worked into a conversation with any leader in your organization you have a chance to visit just as if you are on an elevator together.

Being professional also includes keeping personal details private, associating with others viewed as professional, communicating well, demonstrating a positive attitude, treating others with respect and offering help to others. All of these things will communicate to others that you are competent, someone with a strong character and a high level of commitment. Your professional image will develop over time, so be aware of what you are communicating about yourself.

TWENTY

Thick Skin

My childhood was pretty good. I had parents and brothers who loved me, everything I needed and many things I wanted. I wasn't sheltered or naïve, but I was very comfortable. As I mentioned earlier, I worked in social services before I entered the business world. My experience working with female juvenile offenders quickly and sadly taught me that I grew up in a very different reality from these girls. I was truly shocked by the stories they told me and by their life experiences at such a young age. I could never show my worry or sadness for them, as it was important that they believed we could tackle anything. I had to master my poker face, because it was in their best interest that I did so. Today, I still use that skill when people shock me. My background in social services birthed my thick skin.

In the business world, you will likely encounter people who are difficult to work with. They might be rude; they may just be ignorant; they might be threatened by you. They might have poor impulse control and use disrespectful language or they could be outwardly aggressive or vindictive. When handling the challenges, you really have two choices and both are appropriate depending on the situation. You can hold your ground while being polite or be more assertive and aggressive to defend yourself. The first step is to decide if the person is habitually rude or whether this is an isolated episode. The second thing to do is to not get emotionally upset. Even if the difficult person cannot control his or her behavior, you can control your emotions and you should. Don't get sucked into unprofessional behavior. That said, if the behavior is constantly rude and continuous and is impacting your ability to your job, then it is a chronic situation you must address. Here are the types of difficult people you might encounter in the business world:

- **Steamroller**: inflexible, "my way or the highway."
- **Monopolizer**: takes over the task without allowing input from others.
- **Underhanded**: makes snide remarks, trivializes others comments.
- **"No" person**: a negative person who thinks nothing will work.
- **"Yes" person**: agrees with everything and volunteers everything but accomplishes nothing.
- **Silent**: gives no feedback, comments or ideas.

Some people are simply not worth your time and

energy to deal with. Some people are who they are and won't change. Sometimes, we simply have to "pick our battles." But if the situation or behavior persists and you do need to address it, then you should follow these steps:

- **Keep your cool**: remain calm and don't overreact to a particular situation. Don't get dragged down to the negativity of the other person.
- **Gather your thoughts**: if you are in the middle of a conversation that is upsetting, ask the person to repeat or clarify their question or comment even if you know exactly what they are saying. This gives you a moment to gather your thoughts and think about your response.
- **Focus your energy on problem solving**: do not internalizing the conflict. Identify the real issue and offer a few different solutions.
- **Separate the person from the issue**: think about the problem to be solved rather than the personality of the other person.
- **Have the conversation in person**: people are usually nicer face-to-face than over the phone or an email, and a personal conversation often leads to fewer misunderstandings.
- **Disarm unreasonable and difficult behavior**: kindness and humor can lighten a situation.
- **Stand up to bullies, but do so professionally**: don't imply you agree with complaints and

don't remain silent which might imply to agree. Counter extremes with facts – negative people often use extremes like "never" and "always."

Business is a web of relationships, and most will be good. When you encounter difficult people, remember it is definitely possible to turn them into your friend. It has been my experience that these people are just testing you and when you get past their difficult front, they become loyal allies. It's easy to take it personally and put up a wall, but don't do that. It shows thin skin. Women show thin skin by crying, withholding information, using the silent treatment, being passive aggressive and holding grudges. Don't take business conflict personally. If you do, it will turn into an ongoing interpersonal conflict. It will result in mistrust, destructive dialogue and cause you unneeded stress, tension and anxiety which will negatively impact your mood and disposition. When you encounter difficult people, keep you cool, think the situation through and address it. You will come out stronger for it.

TWENTY-ONE

There's No Crying In Business

Tom Hanks starred in *A League of Their Own* in 1992 with Madonna, Geena Davis and Rosie O'Donnell. The movie was about a professional female baseball team during World War II. While many American men were fighting the war overseas, the All American Girl's Professional Baseball League flourished in the United States. The movie is a fictional account of that history told through the eyes of two sisters playing for the same team. In one of the most famous scenes, Coach Jimmy Dugan, played by Tom Hanks, gives one of the players a hard time about how she was playing. She can't handle the criticism and starts crying. Then the coach screams the now famous line, "Are you crying? Are you crying? There's no crying! There's no crying in baseball!"

Like baseball, there's no crying in business. And, this is tough for women because we cry when we feel overly criticized, unfairly burdened, undervalued or simply overwhelmed. Women and men are biologically different creatures. Women are hard-wired differently and *four times more likely to cry* than men. Our tear ducts are larger and we have six times more prolactin (the hormone that controls tears) than men. For women tears act as a signal that something is wrong when we are over-worked, sick, angry or frustrated. Tears are not signs of incompetence or weakness but men view them as such. Embarrassment will inevitably follow if/when you lose control and tears flow, especially in front of your manager. Earning back a perception of strength and competence can be a challenge.

So, when you feel the tears coming, what should you do?

- **Focus on your breathing**: make yourself take ten slow, deep breaths.
- **Take a step back**: actually remove yourself from the situation (politely and calmly) if you can. Go to the bathroom or find another private place where you can calm yourself down.
- **Distract yourself**: write notes, dig your nails into the palms of your hands, press your tongue to the roof of your mouth, do your Kegel exercises. Find an invisible way to exert energy and reverse the raw immediacy of your feelings.
- **Take a sip of water**: soothe a lump in your throat or a quivering lip that starts to appear.
- **Take a break**: if a short melt-down won't cover it, then take a longer break and leave the office for 30 minutes.

It's awkward and uncomfortable for both men and women to deal with colleagues who are crying. While the emotions might be justified, you cannot cry publicly. Crying needs to done in private. There is no benefit to having a breakdown in front of others. But, if it happens, if the tears start falling before you can escape, then excuse yourself immediately and calmly, with as much grace as possible. Temporarily removing yourself from the situation gives you time to regain composure. Once you have done that, focus on *solving the problem* rather than dwelling on the emotions you are feeling.

A stressful meeting, a terrible boss, a bad breakup – each of these stressors can legitimately make women feel bad. But crying in the workplace will hurt your ability to fit in with your organization. Tears are interpreted as weak, and a person who cries is viewed as someone who can't handle pressure, or as someone who is manipulative, melodramatic or immature. Crying is a natural and even a healthy release, just keep it private. If you do break down at the office, acknowledge the emotion or circumstance that lead to your outburst. Don't apologize for it; just move on.

TWENTY-TWO

Managing Emotions

Crying isn't the only emotional expression women should consciously manage in the business world. Common sense tells us that people who understand and handle emotions well make better leaders. Good leaders manage stress, remain calm with conflict, enjoy happiness and inspire others, but negative emotions exist. They can even be healthy if they drive us to make changes and stand up for ourselves, but we have to manage them correctly and express ourselves appropriately.

Emotional intelligence is the ability to recognize and organize one's own and other people's emotions and behavior in complex social settings. Four traits are associated with emotional intelligence.

- Self-awareness is the capacity to read one's own emotions which makes a person better at assessing personal strengths and weaknesses.
- Self-management means a person does not let moods and emotions disrupt honest and

straightforward relationships.

- Social awareness means a person can read the emotions and reactions of others and adapt accordingly.
- Relationship management is about using clear, concise communication, kindness and humor to build strong relationships.

Each of these traits can be learned and improved upon to build social capital.

When it comes to managing emotions in the business world, women are known to be more emotionally intelligent, yet we know that displaying emotions is negatively viewed. Again I will defend women by saying that women and men just handle emotions differently. We all know that has implications in our personal lives but it has also been a real barrier for women in our professional lives as well. Negative and high-intensity emotions such as frustration, worry, anger or disappointment can lead to feelings of being overwhelmed. These significant emotions differ between men and women.

Negative feelings such as anger and aggression are more commonly discussed regarding men, but women have these same feelings too, although we experience these emotions differently. As children boys are taught that anger is okay, but girls are taught that anger is unpleasant and not lady-like. As children turn into adults, men are more comfortable expressing their anger on the spot so male anger is viewed by others as situational. Women tend to hold anger in so female anger looks more internal, like the emotions have over-taken her. When we feel angry at work, it is very important that we don't appear overly emotional. Maybe a client or co-worker snapped at you unfairly, a passion project got canceled unexpectedly, maybe a colleague lost her leadership role or your department is facing reorganization. You will have real situations at work that make you frustrated, worried, angry or disappointed. If you handle these situations poorly, your professional reputation will be damaged.

When dealing with negative emotions, several strategies can help you. My favorite is to "respond" versus "react". When I become upset, I stop and evaluate what is happening and how I am feeling. A calculated thoughtful *response* to any upsetting situation offers me a better conclusion than a defensive, emotional, immediate *reaction*. A response is more thoughtful and logical and usually results in more progress to solve the problem. I learned this concept at one of my first sales training classes and I have used it so much that people think I am calm and unflappable. I do not always feel that way on the inside, but I have learned to diminish my reactions. Now, when I do have a strong reaction to something people really notice that I am upset. Even when I think my behavior only mildly demonstrates my frustration, my team becomes very nervous and worried because they rarely see me displaying frustration of any kind.

Another way to help with negative emotions is to stop feeding them. Surround yourself with positive people instead of people who "borrow trouble" or have a negative attitude. If co-workers are gathered around the break room in a gripe session, then do not go in to the break room and feed the negativity. Surround yourself with positive people to help keep the negative feelings away.

Feelings do not develop immediately, they build. Recognizing your emotions as they are developing is another important aspect of controlling negative feelings. You should know your own warning signs. Does your mind go blank? Do you shake? Does your breathing change? Do you clench your fists or jaw? Recognizing the feelings while you can control them allows you to manage your response and not react. Do you need to take a break? Do you need to relax? There are many simple relaxation exercises that can calm your emotions and give you time to think through your response. Deep breathing, slowly repeating a calming word or phrase, using positive imagery and slow, non-strenuous exercises such as yoga poses are some of the techniques you can use to soothe yourself when you feel the pressure mounting.

Tied to emotions is disposition. And women tend to have a natural disposition toward kindness which can be helpful at the office. While my career has included roles in operations and marketing, most of my background has been in sales. When I started my career, my long term goal was to become a Key Account Manager (KAM). KAMs manage our business with our largest (key) customers, and I thought it would take a decade to rise to that level. I became a KAM after only two years. Meeting my first large, strategic customer was slightly nerve-wracking but also exciting. I was surprised and disappointed when he said, "You are too nice to be in this business." What?

Kindness is good for business especially in today's world where people are increasingly less connected due to technology. No matter what industry you work in, relationships build business. The best way to build relationships is to be kind and compassionate which builds trust, and trust builds business relationships. In *Creating WE*, a book about building healthy organizations, author Judith Glaser explains that when someone is kind and respectful to us, our brains produce more oxytocin and dopamine, which helps us, relax, feel open to others and become more sharing and cooperative. When we feel threatened or disrespected teamwork and productivity suffer and workplace relationships suffer. Many studies show that workplace burn-out actually comes from employees feeling a lack of caring and compassion from the company.

A female's naturally caring, empathetic and compassionate disposition benefits the business world and emotional expression does not automatically have to make the workplace uncomfortable. Monitor and control your negative feelings so that they do not become negative for your career and use your positive female disposition to foster a healthy corporate culture in your workplace.

TWENTY-THREE

Being A "Woman"

It took me a while to figure this one out. As a young female moving through the business world, I found it really confusing and challenging to be a woman and a vendor. As a female it is appropriate for men to do chivalrous things like open doors for me and pay the tab, but as a vendor I should open the doors for my customers and I should pay the tab. When I started on my career journey I did not know how to balance these two identities, and I made a lot of mistakes. Now, it is very clear to me. I am a vendor, not a woman.

I work in the Midwest where it is very much a "good old boy world". Early on it was hard for me to break some of the barriers; I was always an outsider. So when a high-level customer asked me to a happy hour, I was excited. I was being invited into the clique; women were never asked to happy hours. I was very proud of my invitation to be a part of the club, and I happily went the "meeting". And that first time, I picked up the tab because I was the vendor after all. But then the next time the customer paid the tab and explained to me that each time we got together we rotated who paid. This actually pleased me because I thought I was part of the club. Not only did they include me but I didn't even have to pay for everyone. So, I continued to participate in the happy hours, and everything was great. During those times, I gained great insights into my customer's organization and learned more about how that retailer operated. Then, the ringleader of the happy hour club invited me to lunch. My intuition kicked in, and I had a funny, uncomfortable feeling. When I arrived at the restaurant, my concern was confirmed. This was not a business lunch. This was a personal lunch, and I realized quickly that I had blurred the lines by participating in the happy hours. The gentleman hadn't invited me to happy hour because he and his associates wanted to be my business friend. He invited me to happy hour because he saw me as a woman instead of a business colleague.

Whenever I have allowed a business colleague to see me as a woman instead of a business colleague, I have regretted it. It has created the opportunity for a sexual advance that I wasn't prepared for. Business relationships with men are just that – business. I still go to happy hour with customers, but I always pay the tab. As a female, making business relationships personal comes with risk. I make it my responsibility to earn their respect through my work. Whenever I have handled myself correctly and maintained professional boundaries, my male business friends have always treated me with dignity and respect.

TWENTY-FOUR

The Wives

What is it about women? We can be horrible to each other or the very best allies. We encounter other women in the business world as subordinates, peers, customers and superiors. We also encounter women who are the wives of our male subordinates, peers, customers and superiors, and I can promise you that your career will not go far if you still interact with other females the way many of us did in middle school. Like our girlfriends and other female counterparts in those drama filled years, the wives are tricky.

For the most part, I have been blessed to work with great men: fun, kind and family oriented colleagues who I genuinely consider to be friends. I did not understand the dynamics of the wives until my friend Sandi casually mentioned it to me after a Christmas party. I commented that one of our male peers had been surprisingly antisocial, and she nonchalantly reported, "That's just because his wife was there. The men never talk to me either when their wives are around." I thought that was so strange, because he and I were just friends. There was no reason for him to avoid me because of his wife. Why would his wife think something inappropriate was going on between us, when nothing inappropriate was going on? But, Sandi was right. Men always act differently when their wives are around. Do not take it personally. The men you work with every day will not be as friendly toward you when she is there, just accept it. And, you should not underestimate the power of the wives. The wives of your leaders, coworkers and customers can block your success if they do not like you.

When the wife of a male coworker or customer is around, be alert to her impression of you and win her over. I always use two simple strategies when the wives are around. First, talk to her, not her husband. Let the man come talk to you; do not give the wife any reason to think you are a problem for her or that she needs to compete with you. This is not the time to build your professional relationship with him. Second, talk to her about family, hers and yours, so she knows you recognize the value of family. Otherwise, just be you, ask questions, get to know her and be genuine. Understand that the men you work with value their families, as they should. Respect them for it and be thankful you work with nice men.

TWENTY-FIVE

Finding Support

As women we like to connect with others. We like to talk about experiences and feelings. This carries over into business, even if we work with more men than women, we need to find support and people to connect with rather than deal with our thoughts in isolation. We will make better decisions and find inspiration and clarity if we can talk things out. There are numerous ways you can find support when you need to vent. Hopefully, there are other females in your professional and personal network, a safe circle of work friends, a mentor and a sponsor. Each of these groups of people can provide support as you navigate through your career.

Networking is important for many reasons. Certainly these new relationships can create business opportunities (sales opportunities, job opportunities, knowledge about current trends, legislative updates, etc.), but it can also lead you to make meaningful personal connections with like-minded people who work in a similar industry. Networking can help you find great business friends. It is one thing to connect with those in your circle of work, but it is also important to stretch beyond it. Joining professional organizations within your industry and supporting community organizations (church, charity, chamber of commerce, etc.) are excellent ways to meet other professionals. These people can provide business leads and an objective ear.

Long term career success largely depends on professional networking. Simply put, networking describes professionals connecting with other professional and your business network should include a healthy mix of people who fill different roles. When thinking about your network, be strategic and understand that it will develop with time. Your network is also multifaceted with people who help you and people you help.

Bosses, peers, human resources employees, staff from other divisions, subordinates, community members, friends, family, teachers, customers, vendors – all of these people and many others are candidates to become a part of your professional network. But, your network should not be confined to the people you know already. Your professional network should also include people with influence, a bright future, shared interests and similar ambitions. They fill specific roles to further your career development or you fill a role for them:

- **Connectors**: people who introduce you to others and open new channels of relationships for you.
- **Mentors**: more knowledgeable colleagues who know your work and skills and offer feedback

and advice to further your professional development.

- **Nurturers**: those who listen to your ideas and frustrations while offering support and a safe place for honesty.
- **Teachers**: people who help you broaden, practice and master new skills.
- **Informers**: others who have access to information that you don't have and share it with you.
- **Sponsors**: leaders in your organization who support your development publicly and help you gain visibility for advancement.

Spending the time required to build relationships with people who fill these roles is time well spent, and you should provide the same support to develop reciprocal, long lasting connections. The larger your network, the more access you will have to information and resources which increases your self-confidence and professional worth.

As well as finding support when you need it, the mentors and sponsors in your network are important in terms of career advancement. Let's talk more about these two groups of people.

A mentor is another professional with more seniority than you who offers knowledge, wisdom and advice to support your professional development. A mentor supports you by giving feedback, coaching and guiding you with two broad goals – helping you achieve your learning and career goals and building your confidence and self-awareness. Some companies provide official mentor/mentee relationships. If your company does not, you can find your own mentor. It should be a person who understands the environment you work in and your potential to be successful. Four types of mentoring exist, and throughout your career you will likely have each. They might even overlap.

- Informal mentoring evolves naturally when a more experienced person decides to help a less experienced person.
- Positional mentoring occurs when a manager offers support to an employee.
- Formal mentoring programs are created by some organizations to focus on specific objectives like retention or leadership development.
- Situational mentoring happens when short-term support is provided due to changing circumstances, like a new computer system or a structural reorganization in your team or group.

A sponsor provides a very different type of support than a mentor. Good advice from a mentor inspires and coaches you to improve in ways that might lead to a promotion, but a sponsor actually gets you promoted. Like a mentor, a sponsor will give you feedback, but a sponsor also knows your ambitions, believes in your ability and has the power to advance your career with promotions or special projects. A sponsor is invested in your professional development; he or she bets on you and looks bad if you fail. In a large company, a sponsor would be two or more levels above you. In a small company, the owner or president would be a potential sponsor. You can open the door to sponsorship the same as when looking for a mentor; simply ask a leader in your organization for a meeting, tell the person your professional goals and ask for feedback. Then be open and respectful to what you hear and deliver results based on the feedback received. Finding a sponsor to advocate on your behalf is easier said than done. Sponsorship is earned and only happens if the sponsor trusts you. Sponsorship isn't formal, it develops over time.

At my office, there is also a small group of people who I think of as my "safe circle." They have earned my trust over the years. I can talk with them, vent to them, be truthful about challenges. I can relax around them and take off my "corporate" face. I am safe with these people, even with all of my imperfections. I can even express my emotions without repercussions. These people are rare and few, but I value them more than any of the other people I turn to for support. I hope you can develop a "safe circle" of trusted colleagues.

Business women today have many ways to find professional support. Networking within your organization and within your professional and local community, finding mentors, earning sponsors and developing a safe circle of business colleagues can all provide you with professional development and emotional support.

TWENTY-SIX

Make Life Easier

A common topic young women want to discuss is work-life balance, and rightfully so because work-life imbalance can cause tension at home, sleep-deprivation, alcohol and tobacco use as well as other problems. It isn't easy for men or women, but the problems are compounded for professional women. We often feel guilty for our inability to "do it all," and our family responsibilities are often blamed for women being unable or unwilling to move their careers forward.

So, how can you manage all of the demands of your career and home? First, you must take care of yourself. You have to be refreshed, centered and energized in order to give your work the depth of attention it deserves. Much like when you are on an airplane and the flight crew reminds you to put on your oxygen mask before helping others, you have to be together yourself in order to benefit anyone else. Business demands can drain you, so be smart about how you prioritize and be efficient with your time. What can be done tomorrow? And what will be done better tomorrow if you are rested, ready-to-go and not resentful of having so many things to do?

For me, the stress of too many things to do triggers anxiety, so I have developed some tactics to reduce the number of tasks I need to get done in a day, week, month or year. Here are some tips that have made my life easier:

- Plan your day. Do the most important or most difficult task first and set your break times and office departure time. Include both the professional and personal things you need to do and do personal tasks on your breaks when possible.
- Schedule fixed personal time to work-out, pay your bills, meditate, whatever it is you need to do.
- Include everything on *one* calendar, business and personal appointments, as well as key dates.
- When it's time to run errands, run them all at once and map it out before you go. Be efficient.
- Keep healthy snacks in your desk and your car. This will allow you to avoid unhealthy office vending machines and drive-thru restaurants but still have something to nourish and energize you in your stomach when you need it.
- Leave a notepad and business cards in your car and work bag. These business basics should always be readily available to you when you

need to rush into a meeting, especially if you didn't have the time to completely prepare.

- Disconnect when you need to focus. Turn off your phone and close your email when you are preparing for an important meeting.

- Delegate the tasks that are less important or do not fit your strengths. Save your time for the priorities and do not waste time doing things that someone else can do faster or better.

- Cook ahead, divide meals into the portions you need and freeze them. This will ease the burden of weeknight cooking and help you avoid eating out which is expensive and often unhealthy.

- Wash lettuce, carrots, celery and other vegetables and put them in zip lock bags with a damp paper towel. These single sized servings will remain crisp and be easy to grab-and-go.

Pre-sort the laundry. Keep two laundry baskets, one for lights and one for darks, and then put them directly into the washer.

Do the same thing when you are returning from a trip. Organize your dirty clothes, lights and darks, so you can just drop them off in your laundry room, ready to be washed.

- Keep an on-going shopping list that the whole family uses to write down anything that needs to be purchased: food, drug store, school supplies, etc.

- Get a cleaning *person* (not a cleaning company). The employees working for a cleaning company have no personal attachment to you or your home. Every poor experience I have had with cleaning services has been with a cleaning company, but my cleaning ladies have been invaluable, helping me keep my personal life orderly.

- Hire a lawn service. In the Midwest, lawns require weekly attention March through October. This saves me up to three hours a week, but I can still work outside on weekends when I want to.

- If you have pets, use a pet sitter instead of a kennel. This saves you trips to drop off and pick up, is usually less expensive and your pet would probably rather stay home anyway.

- Only buy dishes that go in the dishwasher.

- If your job allows it, work from home every once in a while. On days I am able to work from home, I am super productive. I have no travel time and fewer interruptions. I am able to get a great amount of work done in a short amount of time, especially detail oriented projects that are easier to complete without interruptions. Working from home also helps personally because instead of taking a break to chat with a coworker, I can do the dishes or laundry, and I don't even have to spend time putting on my make-up.

- Traveling a lot? Use your free nights on the road for hard-to-schedule "me" time. Go to the spa, enjoy a nice meal, catch up on phone calls with friends and family, see a movie, exercise or relax. Do whatever you need rejuvenate your mind, body and/or spirit.

- Join Costco or Sam's Club. Bulk buying and keeping your freezer stocked reduces the number of times you have to shop. If you can, use e-commerce to have grocery and basic supplies delivered to your house on a regular basis.

- If possible, have a second freezer in your garage or basement loaded with homemade soups and other meals that you can quickly and easily grab for a weeknight meal.

- Take your vacations! You need this time to rest, refresh and focus on your personal life.

Good childcare is an absolute priority. Without that, it's impossible to fully focus on the job. As a single mom, I've used different kinds of support over the years. My ex-husband, my mom and other family members have always been a great back-up team for me, but I have also used traditional day care centers, employed a nanny, and even with my daughter in high school today, I still use a nanny service occasionally when work requires overnight travel. I have never allowed childcare to be a reason I could not do whatever my job required. I have always figured it out, and I have done that many different ways over the years.

That being said, businesses are recognizing that we

have real lives. A new buzzword at our company is "flexible productivity." As leaders we talk with our employees about ways to better integrate our business and personal lives. We develop meaningful, *individualized* solutions that enable employees to perform at a higher level and manage their personal and professional needs. For example, I might agree to allow an employee to leave two hours early each Wednesday to coach his child's basketball team, knowing that he will come in an hour earlier each Tuesday and Friday. Working cooperatively assures professionalism and employee investment.

I learned the trick of flexible productivity long before it was a buzzword. I figured out early in my career that getting things done prevented "burn-out." It's easy to focus on the never-ending list of things to do for my job, but when my personal tasks were not getting done, I got very frustrated. But, with each role, the way I achieve work-life balance changed. I have managed it several ways over the years depending on what worked with my business responsibilities. In some positions I've held, it worked better to do personal things in the morning before my work day started. In other roles, the lunch hour was a great time to take care of personal errands. Today, technology makes it much easier to balance business and personal priorities because I really can work anytime from anywhere. I just need my laptop and a connection. That is great for flexible productivity. Even so, I carry a jumbled list of priorities every day and I have a crazy calendar. Generally speaking, when I am not traveling for business, I work from 7:30 a.m. to 5:00 p.m. but in truth I look at my day as a 16 hour block to get everything done, and I am constantly juggling and reprioritizing. Life is like that.

Managing your calendar is critical to making life easier. Try never to let your calendar manage you. Here are some helpful tips for managing your time wisely:

- **Check your calendar first**: review your calendar at the beginning of both each week and each day to make sure you are prepared for your upcoming meetings and recall all of your commitments.

- **Consolidate**: as previously mentioned, use one calendar as the central place for your schedule incorporating both business and personal appointments. This will help you prioritize each day and prevent double-booking yourself.

- **Share**: sharing your calendar with employees, coworkers and family will make your life easier. People who need to make appointments for and with you can work around your schedule if they have it. You can still keep personal appointments private with Outlook features or your own personal system.

- **Separate appointments from tasks**: add appointments to your calendar, but don't mix them with your To-Do List. Keeping your tasks separate will keep your mind clear.

- **Streamline your schedule**: when you need to set up a meeting or social event with more than one person, use an online scheduling tool like Outlook or other software instead of sending email messages or making phone calls. This will eliminate the constant back and forth communication.

- **Focus**: include all pertinent information in the notes of the Outlook appointment (travel details, event details, etc.) so you can always find the information.
- **Color-code**: highlight appointments in a different color so they stand out: work, family, medical, vacations, etc.
- **Get your (beauty) sleep**: sleep improves memory, curbs inflammation, spurs creativity, helps you focus, lowers stress and just makes you feel better. Make sleep a priority.
- **Reserve time for you**: whether it is personal appointments, going to the gym or just office time that you need, schedule it for yourself!

No matter how well you manage the intersecting pieces of your day, expect that life will throw some curve balls. You or your family will experience personal struggles such as illness or divorce, events that will pull your energy and focus away from work. When this happens, maintain your professionalism. You may need to share what's happening with your boss to explain your changing work habits or request an alternate schedule, but work is not the place to air out your personal crisis. You will need your boss' support and patience but your real support system should be outside of the office. Keep these three things in mind when dealing with a personal crisis at work:

- Your boss is your employer: your boss is not your friend or therapist. Don't blur the lines.
- Communicate a timeline: most crises have to do with change or loss and it will take time to regroup. Be honest with your boss about what you are facing while being reasonable about the exceptions you are requesting.
- Check in occasionally: communicate changes to your timeline and update your boss on the progress you are making to return to your full work schedule/out load.

Making life easier is an important goal when seeking to excel in the workplace. Use the tricks that help with regular household tasks and to balance business and personal priorities. Make sure you have a back-up childcare plan if needed, that you control your calendar and can handle personal crisis that may come your way. It is all manageable.

TWENTY-SEVEN

Two Drink Max!

This rule comes from Patti Stanger, the Millionaire Matchmaker. On her popular cable T.V. show she includes a two drink maximum in her "Ten Commandments of Dating." Patti believes that drinking makes people lose clarity, let inhibitions go, and inevitably act foolishly. A drink or two can help you relax but won't make you do or say things you wouldn't normally do or say.

I have learned the hard way that it's also a great rule in business. Years ago when I was starting my career journey, I was at an annual meeting. A cocktail party preceded a formal dinner. I was with my team having a great time and enjoyed several glasses of wine at the cocktail party. Unknown to me, there was assigned seating at dinner that night, and I was to be seated beside the CEO of our company. I recognized this was an honor. Senior leaders always sit by other senior leaders or by future leaders who they want to get to know better. It signaled that I was regarded as a future leader in the organization, but now I had had too many glasses of wine at the cocktail party. I was afraid to speak to the CEO during dinner because I feared I would slur my words. Fortunately for me, he was speaking that night so he spent the first half of the dinner reviewing his notes and preparing for his speech, not enjoying table-talk. That was a lucky break for me. It gave me time to drink water, eat food, sober up and think of some intelligent questions and comments I could use in my conversation with the CEO when he was ready to speak with me. The evening turned out fine, but I really regretted almost messing up my opportunity by having so much wine earlier. My teammates could not wait to see me afterwards to give a hard time about my error in judgment (playful banter of course).

Another time I was at a party with co-workers and we were drinking and having a great time. While it's one of my funniest memories, one of my colleagues may not be proud of the fact that he was rapping to "Baby Got Back" and twerking long before Miley Cyrus. It was all in good fun, but this really wasn't appropriate corporate behavior and with the wrong group of people, it could have been detrimental to my friend's career.

You may find a time when you are invited to a "boondoggle." A boondoggle is a work activity that is really pointless but has the appearance of value. In my industry, these consist of "boys" outings, such as hunting or fishing trips that involve overnights of heavy drinking, no wives and very little business. Do not fool yourself; you cannot be "one of the boys" and you cannot win in these situations. You can handle a golf outing, a concert or a professional ball game, but you have no business attending any overnight outing that involves heavy drinking. Politely decline any invitation to a boondoggle.

I have always been lucky to work alongside great team members, male and female, who were trustworthy and generally cared about me as a person. I hope that is your experience as well, but you have to play it smart. Today I have a very small circle of people that I trust enough to really let go with. Patti's two drink rule for dating is also correct for business and a two drink max will keep you out of trouble.

TWENTY-EIGHT

Avoiding Sexual Advances

Any father of a teenage girl will tell you he worries about teenage boys because they have just one thing on their minds. Dads know because they were once teenage boys. Most boys get better at managing their sexual impulses as they grow into men, but some men still act like teenage boys. Businesses now train their male employees on issues of sensitivity, but unwanted sexual advances persist. This conversation is not about sexual harassment. This conversation is about protecting yourself from an unwanted advance. It is about sending a clear message to the men you work with that your relationship is platonic and will not turn sexual. You can communicate using your verbal and non-verbal skills that you are not open to an advance to prevent an uncomfortable situation from happening. You know how to flirt when you want to, right? This is the opposite.

I made many mistakes in this area during the first decade of my career. I put myself in too many uncomfortable situations because I did not know how to politely create the boundary that should have been there anyway. Here's how you can establish the boundaries:

- Remember the "Two Drink Max" rule.
- Dress professionally. No short skirts or form fitting outfits; nothing suggestive should ever be worn at the office.
- Use eye contact only when speaking or listening, too much eye contact can be interpreted as flirting.
- Do not open up too much about personal business.
- If someone flirts, do not flirt back – block it, do not engage, change the topic or bring someone else into the conversation.
- Do not appear available. Talk about your boyfriend or a male friend who could be interpreted as a boyfriend.
- Use closed body language. Fold arms or lean away.
- Ignore emails, texts and calls not related to work.
- Minimize one-on-one time to limit the opportunity for an advance.
- Listen to your intuition.

Avoiding flirtatious behavior and the opportunity for a sexual advance to be made will protect you because you are sending clear messages. It is disappointing that we cannot have fun, unguarded relationships with all of our male counterparts, customers, clients and leaders, but it has been my experience that it just does not work. Too many times, I have been excited about a developing business relationship with a man only to be disappointed when they make a sexual advance. Be alert and protect yourself by establishing clear boundaries. If a man does make an unwanted sexual advance, don't worry about being polite or politically correct, just say "no" and move on. At that moment – the moment he makes his move – he is not your customer, he is not your co-worker or your boss; he is simply a man. You can decline his offer like you would decline any other unwanted sexual advance.

TWENTY-NINE

Discrimination And Sexual Harassment

Dave is "scary smart," we used to say. He's also quick-witted and funny. His brilliant mind just works differently than most people's do. He was my boss for many years, and he is still my friend today. Because he was so quick-witted and funny, I never knew what he was going to say. Sometimes his jokes and analogies were slightly inappropriate, but even if they were off-color, they were never delivered with disrespect, disdain or cruelty toward anyone. They were just funny. Sometimes, when I walked into Dave's office, he would stop in the middle of a story or discussion or joke, and I would jokingly complain to him that he could not change the conversation just because I walk into the room. I would claim that he was discriminating against me, that I should have the same access to information as everyone else in the organization. Then he would say, "Yes, but I've been to enough sensitivity classes to know the consequences of discrimination charges and sexual harassment charges. If I finish my story, that could be sexual harassment, so I'm just not going to speak."

And, he would *never* tell me the story. This was the basis of kidding between us for the decade we worked together, but I secretly appreciated the fact the real reason he never told those stories around me was because he was simply a gentleman.

Discrimination and sexual harassment are not a joke however. Discrimination refers to a bias against a person which results in an employer hiring, firing, failing to promote, offering adverse job assignments, changing compensation, benefits or discipline based on a distinction (sex, race, sexual orientation, etc.). Sexual harassment is a form of sex discrimination when unwelcomed sexual advances, requests for sexual favors and other verbal or physical conduct of a sexual nature affects a person's employment, interferes with work performance or creates an intimidating, hostile or offensive work environment.

I experienced a hostile work environment early in my career. Not all of the men who worked in that organization were inappropriate, but one leader was. He was always making suggestive and lewd remarks, leering at the women, commenting on the size of their breasts, asking single women if they used birth control, and openly making sexual advances. Pornographic photos of women were actually lying around some offices and posted in some lockers. The work environment was just miserable for the women who were there. Unfortunately, this was well before the term "sexual harassment" was used or understood, and it was not considered inappropriate or illegal. You either accepted the working conditions or you quit your job, so I quit my job. In the 18 month period around the time I left, 24 women left an organization that only had about 300 employees. It's clear there was a problem and shocking leadership didn't identify it. In the early 90s most men simply didn't know how to work with women.

Today, allegations of sexual harassment are monitored by the Fair Employment and Housing Commission. Complaints must be filed within a year of the alleged harassment. When a complaint is filed, the company involved is expected to conduct a confidential and impartial investigation immediately, and then take immediate and corrective action if harassment has occurred -- while protecting the person complaining from retaliation. The investigation is designed to be detailed fact-finding which includes interviews with the person complaining, the accused harasser and others who may have information to share.

Examples of harassment as defined by the Fair Employment and Housing Act include:

- unwanted sexual advances
- offering employment benefits in exchange for sexual favors
- making or threatening reprisals after a negative response to sexual advances
- visual conduct: leering, making sexual gestures, displaying of suggestive objects or pictures, cartoons or posters
- verbal conduct: making or using derogatory comments, epithets, slurs and jokes

- verbal abuse of a sexual nature, graphic verbal commentaries about an individual's body, sexually degrading words used to describe an individual, suggestive or obscene letters, notes or invitations
- physical conduct: touching, impeding or blocking movements, assault

If your attempts to avoid sexual advances don't work, then you must deal with the advance immediately. Say NO clearly and demonstrate that you are offended. This is not the time to be polite. Don't worry about hurting someone's feelings, no matter who he is. Most men know this behavior is out of line and won't be tolerated. Most men will stop when you are clear that nothing is going to happen and that will be the end of it. If it doesn't stop, document what happened while it's fresh in your mind: when and where it happened and if there were any witnesses. Also, document your attempts/actions to stop the unwanted advances. Then file an official complaint with your Human Resources department. Most companies take this sort of misbehavior seriously and will investigate the allegation and address it immediately before you take legal action. And, that is your next step, but you owe the company the opportunity to take corrective action before you seek an attorney.

Discrimination and sexual harassment are deeply disturbing. I hope that I am correct to say that businessmen are smarter today and there is less risk to your career and reputation than when my career began. I know that when I drank too much, and whenever I failed to establish clear boundaries, I put myself at risk. That doesn't mean the men should have made sexual advances, and it doesn't mean that every sexual advance in business is sexual harassment. It just means that as my career progressed, I learned how to avoid the advances by keeping my head clear and by sending unambiguous and firmly platonic messages with my verbal and non-verbal skills. Do your best to avoid the uncomfortable situation, but if it happens, protect yourself by making it clear the advance is unwelcomed. If it happens again, that is sexual harassment and you should document both incidents and report to Human Resources immediately.

THRITY

Safe Travels

I travel quite a bit for my job, but it was not until last year when I took a self-defense class with my teenage daughter that I learned how dangerous airports and hotels can be for women traveling alone. In class we were told that 15% - 30% of all females, regardless of circumstance are likely to be assaulted. Eighty percent of all women assaulted are between the ages of 12 and 34. And, while most of these attacks are committed by a man the victim knows, 90% of the attacks by strangers result in serious harm or death to the woman.

Here are some tips while traveling:

- Tie a bright-colored ribbon to your luggage so you can quickly identify it at the airport and quickly be on your way.

- Arrange to be dropped off and picked up from the airport by someone you know. If you have to drive yourself, park near a well-lit entrance or use a valet service if it is available, limit your length of time walking alone.

- If you take a taxi, use one from the airport or hotel service, not a driver who approaches you and monitor your route with Google maps. I prefer to use Uber over a taxi service now. It's typically less expensive and the GPS tracking makes me feel safer.

- Reserve your hotel room with your first initial and last name only, nothing that would indicate you are a female. Your credit card can use your first initial instead of your full name too.

- Do not accept a room on the ground floor. Floors 3-6 are preferred, and rooms closest to the elevator or to heavy traffic areas are best for safety, but they can be loud.

- Never stay at a hotel with public access to the guestroom floors.

- Never eat alone at the hotel restaurant or bar and charge the tab to your room. This tells a predator you are alone and where to find you.

- Never leave your drink unattended. This offers someone the opportunity to drop a date rape drug into your beverage.

- Never order a "girly" breakfast with a pre-order menu that hangs on the door indicating there is only one guest in the room. Order for two or order a "manly" breakfast on the door-hanger, or order your breakfast via telephone.

- If anyone from the hotel needs to enter your

room, room service or maintenance, while you are there, leave the door open. If they don't really need to enter the room, handle what's needed at the door without the staff member entering.

- Cover the peephole on the door with a post-it note while you are in the room to prevent people from looking in at you.

- Always leave your radio or TV on when you leave your room and hang the "Do Not Disturb" sign on the door so it appears that someone is in the room. You can request maid service while you are at breakfast or just skip the maid service.

- If you find yourself in trouble, FIGHT back, don't cooperate and yell "Fire" instead of "Help" to attract attention.

- Trust your instincts!

Travel can be fun and the work stimulating. Just be smart and be safe.

CONCLUSION

A Bright Future For The Next Generation

Being a successful woman in business is not about acting like a man. Being a successful woman in business is about taking advantage of the strengths you have as a woman and recognizing how those differ from a man's strengths. It's about being yourself, but also fitting in with your organization and standing out amongst your peers. Fitting in and standing out is about being a part of the business culture so that the people who are making decisions about your future consider you to be a part of the team. Superiors will sponsor you for advancement not only if you fit in with the organization but also if you shine as a leader. We must start talking about our challenges as women so we can support each other and move forward together. Here are a few final pieces of advice I would like to share with you:

- **Don't rush, allow yourself time to develop professionally**: learn what each role has to teach you. You are preparing for your future, not your next role. Two years is ideal for each role early in your career, then 3 years as you gain responsibility. You need time to learn, time to make good decisions and time to experience the results of your decisions.

- **Market yourself and approach every day as if it is an interview for your next role**: build your network and seek out new opportunities that interest you so you can demonstrate success and highlight achievements. When seeking new roles, focus on getting noticed by the right superiors. Potential sponsors are watching your performance every day. Many promotions are slated during succession planning. Interviews for promotions are often a formality.

- **Have a flexible plan**: it's important to develop a plan for your career progression, a strategy to give you the opportunity to learn from various roles and opportunities, but it's also important that you are flexible with that plan and take advantage of opportunities that you didn't plan for. Any role or opportunity that helps you expand your knowledge and experience is good for your career. This means you should be willing to move laterally across the corporate ladder. Broad experience makes you desirable, keeps you challenged and furthers your development.

- **Take risks**: the job opportunities that will offer you the most growth are the ones that get you outside of your comfort zone. A robust career path will likely take you into directions you didn't plan.

- Be someone that people want on their team!

We are in a new era where women are better prepared for the business world and more welcomed by men who know how to include us. While confidence, perfectionism and delegating can be challenging for women, our strong communication skills empower us and make us great leaders. Our journey to learn how to better manage personal and business demands will continue, but we will figure it out. Change comes slowly but change happens, and women will continue to progress in the business world. Be a part of it! Do the things that will make you stand out in your organization. Recognize the strengths you have and what others see in you, and forgive yourself for mistakes. Keep moving forward. Success is fun and rewarding. I truly hope that you become an active member of your business environment, participate in the conversations happening within your company and industry and build a future for the women who will follow in your footsteps. The business world needs you!

Special Thanks

I have been blessed throughout my career to work with wonderful men and women who were patient, kind and helpful. I thank them for years of friendship and continuous support. I would especially like to recognize John Barnes for his mentoring, sponsorship *and* friendship.

I'm also grateful to the people who helped me put *Fitting In & Standing Out* together: my editor, Susan Leon; Graphic Designer, Kara Hess, and most deeply to the friends and family who read the book and gave me great feedback before it was published: Ronni Dinkel, Steve Dinkel, Scott Meader, Nancy Pagel, Dave Embree, Jennifer Niehouse, Sheila Ward, Kim Burgess, Amy Thompson and Stacy Goddard. You each touched this book with your insights. Thank you!

Bibliography

Ann, Ronnie. (2009, July 29). "Seven Ways You can Put Emotional Intelligence to Work". www.workcoachcafe.com/2009/07/29/7-ways-you-can-put-emotional-intelligence-to-work/

Brizendine, Louann. The Female Brain. New York: Broadway Books. 2006.

Chua, Celestine. "How to Overcome Perfectionism: 8 Simple Steps". www.personalexcellence.co/blog/perfectionism

Chua, Celestine. "Six Downsides of Perfectionism". www.personalexcellence.co/blog/perfectionism

Chua, Celestine. "Ten Ways to Tell if You are a Perfectionist". www.personalexcellence.co/blog/perfectionism

Deaner, Robert. David Geary, Sandra Ham, and Judy Kruger. (2012, November 28). "Males Play Sports Much More than Females even in the Contemporary US". www.gvsu.edu/gvnow/2012/males-play-sports-much-more-than-females-7343.00000.htm

Gray, John. Men are from Mars, Women are from Venus. New York: Harper, 2012.

Hirsh, Sandra Krebs and Kummerow, Jean M. Introduction to Type in Organizations. United States of America: CPP, Inc., 1998.

Horner, Al. Not Me!. Minneapolis: Bronze Bow Publishing, 2008.

James, Geoffrey. (2012, Octber22). "Six Infallible Ways to Earn Respect". www.inc.com/geoffrey-james/6-infallable-ways-to-earn-respect.html

Kay, Katty and Shipman, Claire. The Confidence Code. New York: Harper Business, 2014.

Goman, Carol Kinsey. "Men and Women and Workplace Communication". www.batimes/articles/men-and-women-and-workplace-communication.html

Krackhardt, David and Hanson, Jeffrey R. (1993, July-August). "Informal Networks: The Company Behind the Chart".

www.hbr.org/1993/07/informal-networks-the-company-behind-the-chart

Krakovsky, Marina. (2013, June 10). "The Psychology of Kindness in the Workplace". www.gsb.stanford.edu/insights/psychology-kindness

Leadership Training Tutorials. "Top 7 Reasons Why Women Business Leaders are Needed". www.leadershiptrainingtutorials.com/leadership/communicating-as-a-leader/top-7-reasons-why-business-leaders-are-needed/

Mackin, Ashley. (2013, July 23). "Harassment: How to handle unsolicited sexual advances". www.lajollalight.com/news/2013/jul/23/harassment-how-to-handle-unsolicites-sexual/

Mind Tools.com. "Successful Delegation: Using the

Power of other People's Help". https://www.mindtools.com/pages/article/newLDR_98.htm

Mitchell, Carol Vallone. Breaking Through "BITCH" – How Women Can Shatter Stereotypes and Lead Fearlessly. Wayne, NJ: Career Press, 2015.

Morgan, James. (2013, October 24). "Women 'better at multitasking' than men, study finds". www.bbc.com/news/science-environment-24645100

Neale, Margaret A. (2013, June 17.) "Why Women Must Ask (The Right Way): Negotiation Advice From Stanford's Margaret A. Neale". www.forbes.com/sites/dailymuse/2013/06/16/why-women-must-ask-the-right-way-negotiation-advice-from-stanfords-margaret-a-neale/#6e3aac451635

Renzetti, Claire M and Curran, Daniel J. Women, Men and Society. United States of America: Allyn and Bacon, 1999.

Robinson, Lyndsie. "7 Reasons Women Gossip".

www.Allwomenstalk.com/7-reasons-women-gossip.

TitleIX.

www.Titleix.info

Wharton University. (2007, April 18). "Managing Emotions in the Workplace: Do Positive and Negative Attitudes Drive Performance?" www.Knowledge.wharton.upenn.edu/article/managing-emotions-in-the-workplace-do-positive-and-negative-attitudes-drive-performance/

Weisman, Renee. Winning in a Man's World. United States of America: Xlibris Corporation, 2008.

Made in the USA
Lexington, KY
11 January 2018